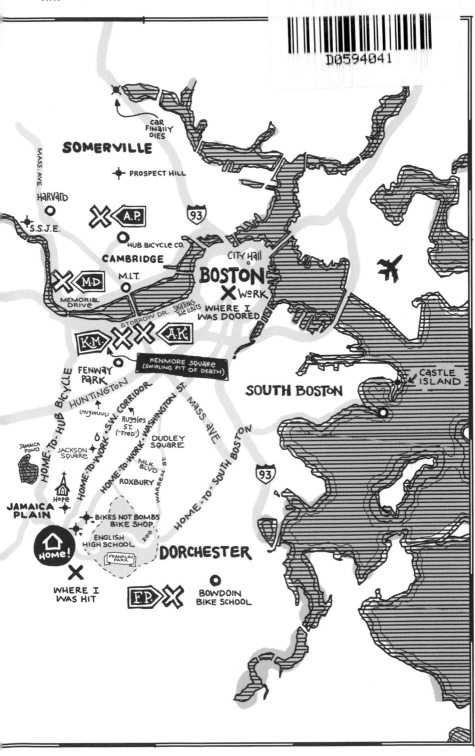

"Simultaneously revelatory and brilliantly accessible, Laura Everett's *Holy Spokes* winds and weaves its way with grace through the little mysteries and miracles of daily life. In this beautiful book she shows us how a single activity—biking through Boston—properly observed, reveals the world. And when we begin to see what we already know, we recall that a generous attention and an open heart can transform even the most mundane tasks into a spiritual practice, occasions to encounter the divine."

— AMY BUTLER
The Riverside Church

"An enlightening spiritual introduction to the art of bicycling. . . . Everett reflects on her bicycling life using a spiritual frame—how to stay true, steer a steady course, find the right gear, know when to pedal, when to brake, and when to rest."

— ELLY BLUE
author of *Bikenomics*

"In *Holy Spokes* Laura Everett offers us the world as viewed from the handlebars of her bike as she navigates Boston's urban landscape, complete with sharrows, greenways, and contemplative aspects of cycling culture. She offers cadence and communion with the world around her as a way of being in a chaotic world. This book is a delight."

— MAX GRINNELL
The Urbanologist

"Even if you don't trade your car for a bike (which you might), reading this book will help you cultivate an awareness that the presence of God is among us—not just in the bright shiny moments but on the pavement, in the mundane, the gritty and the fragile. This intelligent, witty, and thoroughly engaging book will help you remember to practice seeing. Everett is a wise teacher. This is a wonderful book."

— DEBBIE BLUE
author of *Consider the Birds*

"For anyone who has longed to look at the beating heart of their city through the lens of faith, Laura Everett provides a winsome two-wheeled tour. She brings us on an urban immersion experience, helping us pay attention to neighbors as well as neighborhoods, person by person and street by street. What she understands about building community is valuable to faith and community leaders alike."

— WILLIAM H. LAMAR IV
Metropolitan African
Methodist Episcopal Church,
Washington, DC

Holy Spokes

Holy Spokes

*The Search for Urban Spirituality
on Two Wheels*

Laura Everett

Illustrated by

Paul Soupiset

WILLIAM B. EERDMANS PUBLISHING COMPANY

GRAND RAPIDS, MICHIGAN

Wm. B. Eerdmans Publishing Co.
2140 Oak Industrial Drive N.E., Grand Rapids, Michigan 49505
www.eerdmans.com

23 22 21 20 19 18 17   1 2 3 4 5 6 7

ISBN 978-0-8028-7373-6

Library of Congress Cataloging-in-Publication Data

Names: Everett, Laura, 1978– author.
Title: Holy spokes : the search for urban spirituality on two wheels /
    Laura Everett.
Description: Grand Rapids : Eerdmans Publishing Co., 2017. |
    Includes bibliographical references.
Identifiers: LCCN 2016055141 | ISBN 9780802873736
    (hardcover : alk. paper)
Subjects: LCSH: Cities and towns—Religious aspects—Christianity. |
    Cyclists—Religious life.
Classification: LCC BR115.C45 E94 2017 | DDC 248.8/8—dc23
    LC record available at https://lccn.loc.gov/2016055141

Dedication

To Abbi, with whom I vow to always adventure,
&
To Kate, who isn't on a bike. Yet.

Contents

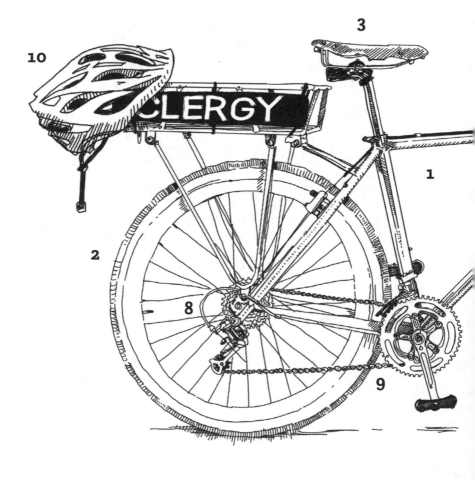

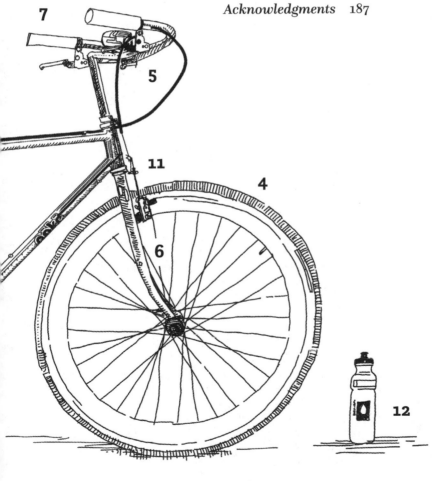

Introduction

Cyclists escape the pain and drudgery of being alive by doing something we love to do, but we can also integrate that thing neatly and practically into our everyday lives. . . . Cycling can be as practical or as frivolous as you want it to be. It is a way of life.

Bike Snob NYC, *Bike Snob*

I've been converted: I am now a cyclist. I started riding a bicycle regularly because my car died, not necessarily to decrease my carbon footprint or to find some deeper, cosmic truths. My cycling conversion was utterly practical. I needed to get around my city.

People don't usually take up bike commuting in search of transcendent wisdom; they choose yoga, running, or maybe even surfing. Bike commuting has not been a traditional path towards enlightenment. And yet, as I bike across the cobblestones and potholes of Boston, I now have daily opportunity to see the life of my city more clearly, love the broken world around me more dearly, and follow this path more nearly.

When I took up cycling as my primary means of transit, my intention was to get around my crowded city. I also hoped I'd get in better shape. Maybe I'd be skinny enough to wear those skinny jeans. I had visions of being one of the cool kids slicing through stopped traffic on my bicycle. I imagined myself moving with the ease of a Dutch cyclist, my skirt flowing in the breeze and flowers in my basket.

The bicycle did all of that. I do get around the city more efficiently, often faster than I would by driving and then trolling for a parking spot. I'm in better shape, though not exactly skinny. (I learned those ubiquitous skinny jeans on cyclists serve a practical function: there's no extra fabric to get caught in the chain.) And I do slice through stopped traffic, though I don't have flowers in my bike basket as often as I imagined. But the bicycle has changed something more fundamental in me, something spiritual—and I was utterly unprepared for that.

It takes intentionality to get on my bike. It's far easier to just walk out the door and get into a car or go to the subway. Instead, every day I pick out clothes that won't get caught in the chain, and check the temperature and weather for my morning commute and my night ride home. I pack my bag with an extra layer in case I'm wrong about the weather, and shoes for a quick change when I get into the office.

From the basement of our old Boston triple-decker, I push open the heavy metal bulkhead from the darkness below and lug my bike up the stairs into the bracing sunlight. Along the narrow path beside the house, I roll along to where sidewalk begins, and onto the pavement below. Then the ritual starts. Attach my bag, check my bike, and check the time again. Helmet on. Sunglasses on. Leg over. Push off into the bright morning. This rhythm, this intentionality of preparation and then movement, has become a daily practice for me.

My commuting route offers remarkable consistency. As I turn off my street onto the main road, the students arriving late to English High School have their earphones in and their eyes on phones, so I move around them, rather than they around me. As I turn onto the bike path, I ride up and over the same cracks where the tree roots are causing the pavement to buckle. Every day I swerve around the inconveniently placed lamppost on Green Street and avoid the puddle that always pools on New Minton Street.

The regularity of my bicycle commute has formed me. If I leave at 7:45 A.M. precisely, I see the same woman with an old-school Walkman and purple Spandex pants walking alongside the bike path, swishing her hips to music only she can hear. I see the same trees go from barren to bursting as the seasons change. My regular route has given me a small piece of land to watch over. I know these potholes and trees and odd people. Seeing them every day allows me to see them change, and in that process, to grow to love them.

That whole "love thy neighbor" thing is a lot easier to do when you actually *see* your neighbors. I know when school is on break because the students aren't in my path. I know when spring is near because I glimpse the buds on the trees—and because the Department of Corrections van begins parking along the bike path, with men in matching uniforms performing their enforced community service by raking the dregs of last year's leaves. By bike, I actually see people and places that I simply didn't notice when I rode by car or train.

My conversion to becoming a cyclist occurred in tandem with my conversion to becoming an urban dweller. The speed of riding a bicycle is perfectly calibrated for learning a city and imbedding a map in your mind. Walking is too slow. Driving a car, like taking the subway, is too fast and too isolated. Cycling through a city requires a steady concentration. On a bicycle, I'm at eye level with the world and can actually see the city around me. That's how the city became mine. I began to start claiming it as my own, history and cracks and wounds and all.

In Boston, history doesn't live far beneath the surface. The city reminds you that it was here before you and it will be here after you. My office window looks out onto the Granary Burial Ground, where Samuel Adams, Paul Revere, Crispus Attucks, and Phyllis Wheatley are buried. On any given day, if my window is open, I can hear a tour guide shout below, "The British are coming! The British are coming!" History is thick here, unavoidable even. We ride on roads that are well worn by all those who have gone before us.

The bike path I take out of my neighborhood is the direct result of 1970s protests against a highway cutting through the city. As I get closer to downtown, I ride the same Boston streets biked by Kittie Knox, a biracial seamstress dressing in men's clothes who managed to beat both men and women in bike races, but died in obscurity in 1900 at twenty-six years old. I ride on Columbus Avenue, the same road where Albert Pope set up his bike shop in the 1890s, providing the first commercially available bicycles in the U.S. Dig down deep enough, and these Boston roads are probably the same ones Paul Revere rode by horse.

Moving through Boston by bike has shown me that the city is a sort of scripture, a holy text to read and reread, to study and memorize, to grieve, to celebrate, and, finally, to make sense of the world. Paying attention and striving to live mindfully as an urban resident forms—or at least invites—certain spiritual practices in me.

I'm not the first or only person to consider bicycles in spiritual terms. Notoriously cranky cyclist and blogger Eben Weiss, otherwise known as Bike Snob, dedicated a book to becoming "The Enlightened Cyclist," claiming "rush hour is ripe for a messiah." In his romp of a global bike acquisition tour entitled *It's All about the Bike: The Pursuit of Happiness on Two Wheels*, Robert Penn writes, "Today I ride to get to work, sometimes for work, to keep fit, to bathe in air and sunshine, to go shopping, to escape when the world is breaking my balls, to savor the physical and emotional fellowship of riding with friends, to travel, to stay sane, to skip bathtime with my kids, for fun, for a moment of grace, occasionally to impress someone, to scare myself and to hear my boy laugh. Sometimes I ride my bicycle just to ride my bicycle. It's a broad church of practical, physical, and emotional reasons with one unifying thing—the bicycle."

There's genuinely something spiritually formative about the daily discipline of cycling, and something transcendent about the experience of riding a bike. To my mind, practical cyclists are both spiritual and religious, that is, they have both *belief* and *practice*. Ask any committed cyclist to tell you why they ride, and you invite a testimonial full of evangelical zeal for the good life available to all who embrace the gospel of cycling.

I believe that God has a preferential option for the urban. But even if I'm right, the challenge of an urban spirituality remains. How do you love the chaos, the decay, the grief? How do you find the holy where the abandoned buildings are not majestic in their ruin but tragic and ugly? How do you find peace in a place where lamppost memorials remember the teenagers who have been shot in the very place where you pause to cross the street? How do you love a place so lonely that we're trained to walk past one another without making eye contact?

Sure, there are glimpses of beauty here. Spring arrives, winter's grip is broken, and birds sing over the rumble of the trains. But each glimpse of beauty is tinged with grime. Just when you think you can't stand winter even one more day, the cold finally breaks, the snow melts. And then trash once hidden beneath the snow is exposed. The anemic grass is littered with plastic liquor bottles, tiny reminders of our isolation where there should be new life.

But this patch of urban grass is where I am. Give me this place and teach me to love all around me. I can't flee to the mountains or retreat to the wilderness every day. And I don't want to. I'm here. And I'm learning to love all of this city, by bike.

In the winter of 1632, a young man named Nicholas Herman had a conversion. During the dead of winter, he stared at a barren tree and somehow saw the possibility of spring. He understood this vision as confirmation of God's grace even within his present desolation. The experience moved him to enter a Carmelite monastery in Paris, where he became Brother Lawrence.

He never became a priest; he didn't have the education. He mostly worked in the monastery kitchen, where he spent a significant portion of his life peeling potatoes. And yet his writing would be collected and become the book *The Practice of the Presence of God,* one of the most revered works of spirituality about cultivating mindfulness in the everyday.

Brother Lawrence lived with the core conviction that everything we do can be done in ways that draw us closer to God. As far as I know, he never rode a bicycle. But even after decades of peeling potatoes, he was convinced that mundane tasks done with intention bring us closer to the holy. He's one of the few spiritual teachers who decided to remain in the middle of the noise of pots and pans and a busy environment in order to develop a deeper internal life and greater attentiveness. I've come to believe that my daily bicycle commute is a way to cultivate that same awareness in me. Maybe. If I pay attention.

My conversion to becoming a cyclist came all at once, in the days after my car died and I began to ride. My conversion to becoming a dedicated urbanist came more slowly.

Boston is not heaven. And no one would confuse the two, especially in the third week of February, when the city is cruel and gray, and the slush gets into my socks on the ride home. But this city and every city, on their best days, offer a foretaste of wildly different and creative communities living side by side.

Boston itself was planted as "a city on a hill," a community both intentionally urban and intentionally religious. We have not yet attained that holy vision of a truly neighborly city. The distance between that holy vision and the current divisions is obscene and growing. But cities on their best days, when the sun is shining and the people are buzzing about in the public parks and in the streets, give a glimmer of what might be, on earth as it is in heaven.

By bicycle, I have become a Bostonian. By bicycle, God willing, I'm learning to be a better neighbor. By bicycle, I'm becoming a velo-evangelist for cities and a distinctly urban spirituality. This is the story of how I'm biking to get there.

Chapter 1

Frame | Rule of Life

There is no manner of life in the world sweeter or more delicious than continual conversation with God.

Brother Lawrence,
Second Letter to Reverend Mother N . . .

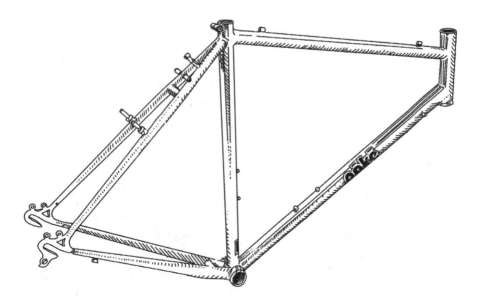

The bicycle, now one of the cheaper and more democratic forms of transit, has a very patrician past. When cycling first began in the United States, you could safely presume a uniformity of gender, race, class, and often religion among those first bicycle owners. Cycling entered the U.S. as a leisure activity primarily if not exclusively of white, Anglo, Protestant men. Prior to around 1896, an average bicycle cost about as much as six months' wages for an average factory worker.

But almost immediately, the social monopoly on bicycles started to break. First, white, married women entered the fray as their husbands' companions on tandem bicycles. Then men from other ethnic backgrounds began to ride. Still, cycling remained a recreational activity for those who had the time and the money to pursue it. It was only when mass manufacturing of bicycles in the United States caused the price to drop dramatically that bicycles became accessible across the socio-economic spectrum. In some ways, the bottom dropped out of the first big cycling boom of the 1890s when cycling stopped being a genteel recreational pursuit of Anglo-Protestants, and became a means of basic transportation for all sorts of other Americans.

In the U.S., cycling has been an urban activity from the beginning. In other countries, rural folks used bicycles as cheap transit to cover long distances, but "the vast majority of early cyclists in America . . . were city people." And that's still true today. Here in the city, a wide range of frames support an even wider range of people. A hundred years ago in Boston, you could assume that cyclists shared certain commonalities. But on the road these days, you can't presume to know the backstory of other cyclists just by eyeing their bikes.

And yet, something about our frames gives us away.

Frames can tell you something pretty quickly about the cost of the bicycle. Steel is sturdy, cheap, and gives a pretty smooth ride, but it's heavy and vulnerable to rust. Aluminum is lighter and won't rust, but it can produce a "harsh ride" because it's less resistant to impact than steel. Carbon fiber is lightweight and excellent at dampening "road buzz," but pricier and difficult to recycle. Yet the frame is only as good as the materials and quality of work put into it. You can purchase a light, crappy, mass-manufactured carbon bike made in China, but get a better ride on a thirty-year-old hand-built steel frame.

In fact, there are frame purists who would never ride anything but a steel-framed bike. Their mantra is "steel is real." These guys (and they do tend to be guys) have probably been riding the same steel frame since the mid-1970s and take a certain pride in bucking trends. These old-school cyclists are known as Freds, and if you make the mistake of asking one of them about steel frames while waiting for a light, you've just invited a fifteen-minute manifesto.

Bicycle frames can also tell us something about gender.

In the early development and popularization of bicycles, people saw their liberating possibility, and some of them got nervous. Suddenly, anyone could travel far of their own volition. For men, that was fine, even productive. But for women, this possibility meant that they could leave the protective sphere of the home, venture into the unknown, and interact with all kinds of people. Instead of sitting delicately at home in their private space, women would be moving their bodies around in public spaces. Somewhat unsurprisingly, this freedom was perceived as a threat; in fact, "for opponents of women's rights, the bicycle exemplified physical and moral danger." The very design of bicycle frames from this era betrays the anxiety about women's bodies and social norms.

Before the introduction of the diamond-framed "safety bicycle," or what we now know as simply the bicycle, men were experimenting with "penny-farthing" or high-wheel bicycles in the late 1870s, while women were relegated to the tricycle. The 1880s tricycle had two large wheels in the rear with a seat in between, and a smaller wheel up front, with pedals below the seat. While men needed a step stool to jump onto their high-wheelers, women could delicately sit lower to the ground and, most importantly, keep their legs together while getting on and off the tricycle and while riding it. Tricycles introduced women to bicycles, and from there, women began advocating for a better ride and less cumbersome clothing. Tricycles moved from being a woman's "intro" bicycle to a child's first bike. High-wheelers faded from popularity as men recognized how unstable and unwieldy they were. And in 1885, the "safety bicycle" was introduced to the market.

When we ride bicycles now, we are essentially riding on the 1880s technology that brought us the safety bicycle. The basic concept of the bicycle has remained relatively unchanged over the past century. Sure, technical innovations have made bicycles lighter, faster, and more comfortable. But specifically, the basics of the diamond frame remain unchanged: wheels of the same size connected by a diamond frame, and a crank connected by a chain to the rear wheel that moves the whole thing along. But women still have the gender presumptions of 1885 built into many bikes. The current step-through frame is essentially the vestige of a bicycle designed so that women could straddle the bike without having their big skirts get in the way or spreading their legs too wide. So when women get on a bicycle, we inherit a whole lot of history with it. These frames orient us, and tether us to a tradition with both good and bad.

Bicycle frames are the structures on which all the rest of our bicycles rest. Made of a wide range of materials—even bamboo—frames are designed for a wide range of cycling activities. A carbon-fiber frame, lightweight and expensive, is great for hundred-mile rides, but not a wise choice for touring, when racks affixed to the front and back carry your tent, sleeping bag, food, and gear. A heavier mountain bike, designed to absorb the reverberations of riding over rocks, adds weight that a city cyclist doesn't need while riding on (relatively) smooth roads. Your frame greatly determines the type of riding you do and the types of components you'll add on. Everything hangs on it. As I slowly joined the tribe of urban practical cyclists, I learned that for many of the "true believers," everything in their lives orients around what they ride. The bicycle becomes a "frame" for the rest of their lives.

Abbi, one of the cyclists I met through the church I attended, explicitly made the decision to take a job at a school a bikable distance away. She had offers from other schools, but picked the one that was far enough away for her to get a daily workout, but not so far that she couldn't reasonably ride. The bicycle was the frame for that and many other decisions in her life.

Historically, monastic communities would call this a "Rule of Life," a set of patterns and norms that govern communal living. The velo-religious live with an implicit Rule of Life, a frame for their particular way of living.

The idea of a Rule of Life originated in the Egyptian Christian monastic communities of the third and fourth centuries. The monastic community of the Society of St. John the Evangelist in Cambridge, Massachusetts, writes, "The word 'rule' derives from a Latin word, *regula*, which implies not so much a system of rules or laws, but rather a way of regulating and regularizing our lives so that we can stay on the path we have set out for ourselves." Practical cyclists aren't so much rule-bound to never take a car or a train or to walk. Rather, in the sense of a "Rule of Life," the bicycle becomes the regularizing frame for other decisions.

For the velo-religious, the frame is strict. How shall we get there? The rule is always "by bike." They make few exceptions for inclement weather; they just wear better rain gear or warmer mittens. The bicycle is their frame for all transit, and then all activity. These people keep kosher.

I didn't begin in the deep end of cycling orthodoxy. At first, my bicycle was nothing more than a replacement vehicle, not some grand orienting principle. But as I rode, I began to see how the framing of a "Rule of Life by bike" was changing how I moved through the world.

Framing one's movement by bicycle opens up certain possibilities and forecloses others. There's a limit to how much you can carry comfortably by bicycle, and so what counts as essential is renegotiated. My grocery purchases have gotten more focused by bike. Bulk toilet paper isn't something I want to bungee-cord to my bike on a rainy day. And no more full gallons of milk for me; instead I purchase a half-gallon. I find myself stopping by the grocery store (which, conveniently, is on my commuter route) more often, but for fewer and smaller items.

Framing one's life by bicycle also means developing a different relationship with time. By bike, I've come to take more seriously how long it takes to get from place to place, and how much effort I need to expend to get there. People who drive cars may also do the same, but transit by car seems so self-evident that many no longer see how their lives are shaped by what a car can or can't do. I hear the strains of this most clearly when I invite friends from the burbs to meet me in the city, and they demur with excuses about how they can never find parking quickly or easily. We've framed most of our movement by car without realizing it.

Framing one's life by bike also means having a different kind of relationship with the weather. As my friend Caroline and I rode home from a nice restaurant one night, we reveled in the perfect cycling weather: cool and dry. Having lived in Mali during her Peace Corps years, Caroline remarked that the village's entire social calendar was weather-dependent. "But here," she said, riding alongside of me, "the only way the weather really affects my life is in how and when I bike." I knew what she meant. Framing my life by bike has created a kind of intimacy with the temperature, dew point, and wind chill—none of which I had considered much before the bike.

In short, the frame of the bike has affected everything in my life, from the mundane detail of how much more sunscreen I need daily, to the transcendent act of having sixty minutes of daily cycling meditation.

While he lived within the Carmelite monastery, Brother Lawrence would have lived under the "Carmelite Rule of St. Albert," one of the shortest monastic "Rules of Life." Most of the twenty-four precepts are about spiritual matters, but others betray a Carmelite practicality in governing their common life, like rule thirteen: "You may have as many asses and mules as you need, however, and may keep a certain amount of livestock or poultry." In this community, Brother Lawrence searched for a rule within his Rule, a "manner of life" that invited the sweet, delicious "continual conversation with God."

As much as my life is now framed by movement by bike, there are others far more observant than I. The velo-orthodox only travel by bike. Their goal is to show that an exclusively bikable world is possible. To prove that everything that can be done by car can be done by bike, some friends of mine recently moved apartments entirely by cargo-bike. A step down in intensity, the velo-conservative use a bicycle for most of their transit needs, but make the occasional exceptions, because it's actually a huge pain to do things like move apartments by bike. There are velo-parents with multiple children packed in either the front wagon or balanced on the back of their bikes. The velo-liberals are the least observant cyclists. Perhaps they ride a bike, but they only do so recreationally. For them, the bike is more of a toy or an occasional form of exercise, not a significant tool that orients their movement in the world. I myself am a solidly observant velo-conservative. Like every religious devotion before it, this group of converts and bicycling evangelists aims to show and then invite others to the comprehensive good life of their religious practice.

For every kind of cyclist, bicycle frames are tools; you want to ride the right one for the right job. Road bikes are for roads. Mountain bikes are for mountains. Mostly this is true. Sometimes it's just an excuse to own multiple bikes. But usually you don't want to ride a bulky cargo bike unless you actually have to carry cargo.

Still, not all frames are being used for their original purpose. Through a rough Boston winter, a mountain bike—with its knobby tires, flat handlebars, and sturdy frame designed to stay upright while rolling over rocks and roots—becomes oddly useful for riding over the snow and ice. The fixed-gear bicycle has become an urban standard, but that's not quite where it started. The fixed-gear bike was the first iteration of the chain drive. Because the gear is fixed, you can't coast. If the bicycle is moving, so are your legs. Fixed-gear bikes, or "fixies," rarely have brakes. They're ideal for racing around a track, because if you're just riding around in a circle, you don't need to brake much. The need for speed has prompted bike builders across the generations to see what they can get rid of to reduce the weight and drag on a bike. So if you don't really need a brake, why add the weight? With fixed-gear bikes, the one gear means that your legs are doing all the work. No alternate gears to down-shift into to get up a hill. Your legs are the gears *and* the brakes.

The fixed-gear is now the go-to bike for the fleet bicycle messengers and wannabes who dart through traffic. It's also pretty fun to ride. Uncluttered with brakes or gears, the frame has a cleanness to it. It's lightweight and feels swift under you. You have a clear sense of your own power on a fixed-gear bike—whatever speed you're getting is because of you, not through some advantage of the gears. What was once designed for time trials in a velodrome is now being used to deliver depositions and screech past a line of waiting cars on the way to the bar. Using bicycle frames for purposes other than their original one betrays an urban scrappiness. The industry gave us a frame; we gave it a new use.

And lo, amid these adaptations, the hybrid bicycle emerged.

The hybrid bicycle is super-easy to make fun of: it's the duck-billed platypus of bicycles. A mash-up of a bunch of bicycle styles, it doesn't do much of anything especially well. And yet, if you're only going to have one bike, a hybrid makes sense for a range of reasons. It isn't prohibitively expensive. It's more stable than a road bike, less bulky than a mountain bike. It's moderately competent at many things, just not spectacular at any *one* thing. Also, the frame is gentle; the geometry is kind. You aren't too hunched over or too stretched out, the way you would be on a road bike. The hybrid frame is designed to be accessible to almost anyone, a sort of one-size-fits-most model.

My primary bicycle now is my commuter, a hybrid of sorts made for the everyday. This is the bike I take out almost all the time. It's a workhorse, designed intentionally to do the things I need it to do. I can lash my computer bag to a rack on the back. The front and rear fenders allow me to ride in work clothes without getting too gritty. The reflective paint job on the frame keeps me visible when I'm coming home in the dark, as the days grow shorter in winter. And it's adaptable. After a cycling injury, I swapped out my drop bars for the courier handlebars that swoop towards my body, allowing me to reach the handlebars with less strain on my back and sit high enough to see the traffic around me. The frame itself is unremarkable, yet just right. Not too heavy to lug up the basement stairs, not so light (and therefore expensive) that I'm afraid to lock it up outside.

About a year after I began cycling, another frame formed, a metaphysical frame, you might say, with a different kind of architecture. I stumbled upon it, really. No longer a total novice, I could ride my bicycle with a certain degree of competence and comfort. I don't believe in riding with headphones; the roads are too complicated, and I need to be able to hear the drivers around me. So, with no music or news piping into my head, I found that, as I rode, my mind would begin to clear, and my deepest thoughts, longings, and even prayers could rise to the surface. I could actually notice the thoughts I was usually moving too quickly to acknowledge. On the bike the sediment in my mind would settle.

Runners, swimmers, and rowers sometimes speak of this—the repetitive motion that allows one's mind to clear. Cycling requires enough motion and coordination that I can't multitask. But at some point the movements and the roads become familiar enough so that I can zone out a bit—and there, in the dependable rhythm and mind-clearing, I have learned to talk to God.

The daily habit of riding a bicycle has done more than

make moments of transcendence possible along my regular route. It has provided a kind of frame of daily meditation and prayer. After a few years on a bike, I found the riding to be regular, unremarkable, routine. And this regularity is exactly what Brother Lawrence suggests for practicing the presence of God. He counsels the seeker to "think often" about God, "in the daytime, at night, in all your occupations, in your exercises, and even during your time of amusement. God is always near to you and with you." Where I had the time and space to think was often on my bike.

And so my time on the bicycle became reflective. My internal conversation became chatty, even. As I came to know Boston's roads better and better, my mind would drift and mull over my prayers. At some point, the road itself started giving me my prayers: the triple-decker house with the foreclosed sign, the roadside shrine to a child killed by a stray gunshot, the despair that seemed to cling to every building on some blocks, the defiant signs of life on others.

Riding a bicycle has made me more prayerful. Riding a bicycle has made me a Bostonian. And while I'm sure this observation might sound odd, with a regularity that has become my urban "Rule of Life," daily bicycle riding has made me more faithful.

Chapter 2

Wheels | Habit

She would like to go more quickly than grace will allow.
One is not a saint all of a sudden.

Brother Lawrence

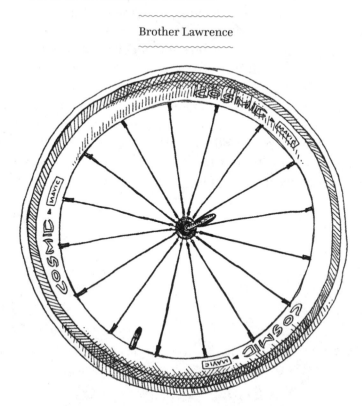

The loss of one set of wheels led me to another set. It was only when my car died that I began to ride a bicycle in the city. Actually, it was my car dying and a good bit of peer pressure.

The first five years I lived in the city, I had a crappy old 1996 Volkswagen Jetta that mostly did its job and not much more. I come from a family where we never bought a car new. Cars weren't something to invest in; the point was to spend just enough to get from point A to point B. Cars weren't status symbols or objects of beauty to polish and preen; cars were sheer utility. Hand-me-downs were totally acceptable. I grew up with my mother driving a whale of a black Plymouth Rambler, a hand-me-down from my great-grandmother. The gas gauge no longer worked, so a spiral notebook lived in the glovebox. Each time one of us refilled the giant tank, we were supposed to record the mileage in hopes of keeping track before the gas ran out. I spent a fair amount of my childhood hours sitting on the side of the road with my mother, waiting for a ride, because a family member had failed to make an accurate mileage entry. This family lesson I learned the hard way: Cars were a necessity of suburban life, but not a joy.

In keeping with family tradition, I attempted to do the minimum to keep my car running. But after finding myself alongside the highway of 93 South on a rainy night when the car stalled out *again*, I had to admit it was over.

I don't know whether it's irony or divine providence that my car died at a time when I was meeting regularly with a group of people for Bible study. These people were more faithful and disciplined than I was. And they carried a conviction that Jesus said far more about justice and money than anything in the Christian culture wars. In the group, we opened our wallets and checkbooks to one another to share how we spent our money, with the goal of developing practices that would help us give more away.

In this small group of seven people, at least three were committed cyclists. With the thin bank account of someone working their first job out of grad school and carrying a fair amount of student debt, I slunk to the Bible study the week after my car died.

"We think you can live without a car. And we can help," they said.

I was skeptical.

I had been formed in suburbia, where life was nearly impossible without a car. Houses were spread out and far from centers of business. Public transportation was non-existent. In our white, middle-class neighborhood of American privilege, cars were a given, like water coming out of the faucet or new stone-washed jeans to start the school year. How would it be possible to live without one?

Many people live in a city without a car, but I hadn't yet and didn't know how, exactly. I began to drag my feet like someone who actually still had a choice about how they moved about, not someone who would be forced to make do out of necessity. Sadly, Jesus never said, "Blessed are you with slight salaries working for a do-gooder non-profit, for you shall inherit a car." More often he was saying, "Look at the birds of the air; they neither sow nor reap nor gather into barns, and yet your heavenly Father feeds them. Are you not of more value than they?" I was worried about getting around.

"Help," I whimpered.

My group came to my rescue. "Angela can teach you how to ride, and Abbi can build you a bike. You don't need a car. We can make this work."

They were right. I really didn't have enough money for even a used car. My subway pass could solve a number of problems in the city, but wouldn't when I needed to travel for work out to the suburbs. My employer at the time, based in the city and vocal on environmental stewardship, still presumed all employees had a car. So my cycling friends and I found Zipcar, a car-sharing service that allowed me to pay by the hour to rent a car from my neighborhood. And then we found my bicycle.

My first adult bicycle was a red-steel Club Fuji bike from the eighties. We first met in an apartment basement, where it lived tucked behind some Christmas decorations and the washing machine. It was a hand-me-down, an old road bike belonging to someone's roommate. I didn't choose this first bike—I took what came cheaply. I paid one hundred dollars for it, and Abbi from Bible study started the repairs. Off came the drop handlebars designed to hunch the rider over into a more compact position, and on went the flat mountain-bike bars to let me sit a bit upright through city traffic. Off came the three-decades old wheels with inconvenient "tubular tires" that are hard to change, and on went some wheels we had ordered off the Internet. Off came the down-tube gear shifters, and on went a single-speed hub, to convert the geared bike into a lighter, single-speed commuter. "Start simple," Abbi told me. "Boston is a relatively flat city. Learn how to ride here without messing with gears."

I figured that if I was going to spend this much time on a bike, it should at least have a name. Because it was built on a Japanese frame, I named it Hideki after a favorite athlete, former New York Yankees outfielder and Japanese baseball star Hideki Matsui. The man's legs were like tree trunks. I hoped that if I rode the bike enough, I'd have impressively strong thighs like him.

I knew how to ride on the quiet suburban streets of New Jersey as a kid, but I had no idea how to ride a bike in a city as an adult. To teach me, Angela led me on my first ride on

Hideki. Abbi and Sandy from Bible study rode behind us, so I was safely sandwiched in the middle. We tried out my route on a Saturday when the traffic was light and the daylight shining. Somehow I had inherited a pack of church-lady bicycle sherpas. They were true believers in bicycles, evangelists eager to show a new cyclist how to ride.

The route from my Boston neighborhood of Jamaica Plain to my office in the center of the city cuts through seven very different neighborhoods: Jamaica Plain, Roxbury, Mission Hill, South End, Chinatown, Downtown Crossing, and Beacon Hill. The bike-commuting route essentially follows the Orange Line subway route, but above ground.

We started our ride on the protected bike paths of the Southwest Corridor, where the most we had to navigate around were pedestrians at stoplights. About four miles in, the bike path dropped out, and we were on city roads, first with a six-foot painted bike lane, and then no bike lane at all. We moved from the protected to the vulnerable in less than thirty minutes.

It was just 6.5 miles from my house to the office. But there, at the end, rose up Beacon Hill.

"Just stay on," Angela said, turning her head over her left shoulder as I trailed behind her. I was breathing hard as I tried to propel my bicycle up a very, very small hill. Angela has only one rule for riding up a hill: Just stay on. You can go as slow as you need to. You can shift down to your smallest gears, if you've got them. But don't get off. As she rode, Angela would chant to herself, "Up, up, up, up!" Now, on days when my life feels utterly overwhelming, when I'm using my commuting time to think of all that I cannot control in my life, I think of Angela's credo: *Just stay on.*

My wheels turned ever slower as we chugged up the embarrassingly small hill. Even now, nearly ten years later, the last bit of my commute up Beacon Hill is a good metric for my fitness. The more time I've spent off the bike, the bigger the hill looms and the longer the ride gets. But when I've been riding frequently, I can zip right up the hill. I feel a particular glee when I'm sneaking up past the cars stuck in traffic, as Duck Boats packed with tourists and school buses full of children gum up the road, and the only space open for movement is in the bike lane.

Finally, we made it to the top. The church-lady bicycle sherpas showed me how to properly lock and tether my bike to the street sign next to my workplace. Then we took one look at my locked office door, turned around, and Angela said, "OK, now do it again—in reverse."

And so I began on my bicycle, slowly creeping towards cycling as my primary means of transportation. Each night I would pack my work clothes in my new pannier hinged to the rack on my bike. Anda, a friend from college who commuted along the wide streets of Washington D.C., gave me the genius tip of carrying baby wipes. The unfortunate truth of bike commuting is that the ride actually requires a significant expenditure of energy and sweat, meaning that cyclists have a reputation that precedes them. Baby wipes help.

I learned to build extra time into my commute for changing clothes. In the beginning, my ride was just a bit too long and sweaty to go entirely in work clothes, especially if I needed to look like an actual adult that day. And so I'd sneak into the bathroom and change: entering clad in Spandex, exiting in a dress and heels as a respectable-ish adult. I felt like a superhero—Clark Kent changing into Superman in a phone booth. And an hour of cardio just built into my day? It was exhilarating! Why hadn't I done this sooner?

But I also had commuting failures, like the times when I

forgot to pack, say, underwear and only had the padded bike shorts I was wearing. And several times during the winter I forgot to pack work shoes, which left me with only the clunkers I rode in. I remember sitting in meetings with a perfectly respectable dress on top, and wool socks and bike shoes peeking out below. The learning curve of bicycle commuting was steep.

This is building habit: Get up, go. Rinse, repeat. Again. Get up, go. Rinse, repeat. Now do it again, in reverse.

My first year of bike commuting required an intentionality that later wouldn't require as much forethought. In the beginning, every bike trip I took meant I had to check out Google maps to review the suggested bike route (which at the time was still in beta). I started bike commuting before the rise of smart phones, which meant I needed to plot my route before I left my computer or carry a paper map with me. I would write out the cues on index cards: Right on Washington St. 1.2m, Washington turns to South St. 0.1m, Left on Belgrade Ave. 1.1m, and so on. En route, I would check my map, check my watch—is this taking too long? Did I miss a turn? Boston is a small city, but with no logical roadways. It probably took me a year of riding every day to really get to know the roads. In the beginning, I had no idea how long it took to get anywhere by bike. My estimates were constantly wrong, which meant I was arriving early or, more often, late through my first year of biking.

When American English speakers try to communicate that something can be picked up again easily after a long absence, they say, "It's like riding a bike." But riding a bike as an adult took far more intentionality than the expression suggests. I hadn't forgotten how to ride, but all the ancillary stuff took building new habits. Brother Lawrence instructs the novice to expect struggles at the start. He writes, "We must not be surprised at failing frequently in the beginning; in the end we will have developed the habit that enables us to produce these acts of love without thinking about them, deriving a great deal of pleasure from them." In my beginning, everything about riding my bike took intention and time: laying out my clothes, finding my lock, pulling together hat and gloves, filling my water bottle, packing my pannier. None of this felt smooth or swift. It would take at least a year before I felt I was just jumping on my bike and going.

Habits are formative, whether good, bad, or somewhere in between. Repeating any action breeds familiarity, which in turn builds a certain dependability. Habits become the surety we fall back on, especially when we're anxious or afraid. I'm as likely to fall back on my habit of biting my fingernails as I am to remember a well-worn prayer. My habit of biking was new to me, but slowly, over that first year of cycling regularly, I needed less and less time to prepare. I needed less and less stuff to get me from place to place, as if having a spare pair of socks or extra bike lights could protect me from the unfamiliar. And at some point over that year, I no longer needed to write out the cue sheet to get from Jamaica Plain to Dorchester Bay. I could just get on my bike and ride.

The habits of our daily life shrink large cities into more manageable places. By traveling the same route each day, I began to see the anonymous mass of thousands become particular. The overwhelming crowds separated into specific people: the football players from English High walking home with the dull thud of their shoulder pads and helmets clunking together; the Muslim faithful speaking dozens of different languages as they made their way to Roxbury Crossing's MTBA station following Friday prayers; Jim and Hannah, regulars at the Egleston Farmers Market, who sell the sweetest Maine blueberries in the summer and the brightest orange squash in the gray of winter; Ann, who no longer used her Vietnamese name, at U.S.A. Dry Cleaners, whose mother was sick and who asked me to pray for her. I only know these particulars because of the rhythm of these regular routes, these habits of commuting through the undifferentiated city.

It's not an especially trendy word, but spiritual habits require *discipline*. Practical cyclists, those of us who ride daily as our primary means of transit, have something any pastor would give her right arm for in her congregation: a discipline and a dedication to the implicit Rule of Life—in this case, Always by Bike. Our bicycles orient our daily life. Our discipline just happens to be on two wheels. We could live another way, but day after day, we make the decision to go by bike, again and again. Around and around, the wheels turn.

A bicycle wheel is actually at least three different components: hub, spokes, and rim. Moving from the inside outward, the hub of the wheel is at the center. The hub is formed by three main parts: an axle around which the whole wheel rotates, internal hub bearings that allow the hub shell to rotate, and an exterior hub shell to which the spokes attach. Spokes are the metal wires connecting the hub to the rim, the metal hoop around the outside. Finally, the tire and the tube (topics for Chapter 4) are connected to the rim.

Around and around it goes. A good bicycle wheel should be consistent all around so the rim is perfectly concentric, a "true" wheel. When a wheel ceases to be consistent, it has become "out of true."

Unlike racing wheels designed to be light, my commuter bike wheels are designed to endure some wear. Bike wheels are fairly sturdy. I rode my first commuter bike pretty hard, the bike and I both banging around. Riding home one night, post-winter, I was breezing past the pothole repair crew that had jammed up the cars on Columbus Avenue. In theory, there's a painted bike lane between the parked cars on the right and the moving cars on the left. But the cars on the left weren't moving that day. In theory, by bike I had a clear path forward, despite the stalled traffic. I was smugly moving past them at a fairly good pace when one of the parked cars on the right pulled out into the bike lane to wedge his way into the stalled traffic on the left. To avoid ramming my bike into his driver-side door, I swerved left—and smack into one of the unrepaired potholes.

I threw on my brakes and put my feet down on the uneven pavement. My front wheel had hit the pothole edge pretty hard—but better that than hitting the car. After a few choice words inviting "You idiot" to "look at the bike lane before you pull out," directed at a closed window and a driver uninterested in my transit tutorial, I walked my bike around the front of the offending car and back into the bike lane.

There appeared to be nothing wrong with my bike or with me. My heart was racing a bit, and I was angry about coming so close to being hit, but I detected no physical damage. Because I was a novice and dusk was falling, I didn't take too long to examine the bike. I was less than three miles from home. So I rode on.

But something felt a bit off. Not horrible, just off. I could pedal and keep moving, but it felt like I was fighting the bike to stay straight. Still, I rode home. And honestly, I rode my bike for the next two days until I could get someone more experienced than I to look it over (not good for the long-term health of your bike). I knew enough to know that something was wrong, but not enough to know what the problem was.

My neighborhood boasts a number of bike shops, each catering to a different community of cyclists: a shop for the young families and old-guy orthodox cyclists, a shop primarily for the bike messengers, and my preferred shop, the one for the commuter class. Bikes Not Bombs is a for-profit shop that funds their non-profit mission. They take donated bikes and rehab them for sale, in the process teaching city kids how to do the repairs. I find them the least intimidating bike shop and the one most oriented towards teaching me what actually is wrong.

With my bike up on the repair stand, the young mechanic spun the front wheel. She stood directly in front of it, her eyes fixed on the space below the fork (which holds the front wheel) where the brake pads hover above the rim. Intently watching from behind her glasses, she said, "Come, look." I bent over to bring my face near hers. "I think your wheel is out of true," she diagnosed.

"See how it wobbles?" she asked. "Let's take it off and check." She flipped open the lever near the caliper on the brake, then flipped open the quick-release lever on the axle and removed the front wheel. We walked to the workbench and placed the wheel on a truing stand, where she started "truing the wheel." An inconsistency on the sides of the rim will result in the brake pad rubbing unintentionally at a point in the rotation, and will make the bike's ride uneven. Many things can cause the inconsistency: hitting the wheel against something like a pothole, an unseen hit like another bike banging into your locked bike, regular wear and tear, a poorly built wheel, spokes that are too tight or too loose, human or mechanical error. To "true" the wheel, the mechanic spun it slowly, her eyes again fixed as she watched for the places of inconsistency. And then, where possible, she made the appropriate adjustments.

This isn't a bad process for humans, either. At its most basic, "truing" is intentionally looking for what's off. We all get out of sorts for our own reasons. Am I over-tired? Have

I been around too many people? Am I hungry? Did someone cut me off today so I hit an emotional pothole? What's actually going on here? Am I really angry at this person, or at something else entirely? For me, first I notice that I'm wobbling. Then I wonder, *Why am I out of alignment?*

Almost every spiritual tradition has some process of self-examination to help us get honest with God and ourselves about what's going on. In the Roman Catholic tradition of spirituality from St. Ignatius of Loyola, people take part in both the daily Ignatian "examen" and the "Spiritual Exercises" designed for a month. The daily examen is something of a quick check-in before one leaves the house and begins the day; the intensive Spiritual Exercises are a more in-depth cleanse and overhaul.

I appreciate the tradition in some churches of naming *all* the "deadly sins," just in case you may have done something that you've forgotten about during your self-reflection. To me it feels like going through a checklist of bike repairs, jogging my memory of the ways I've been bent out of sorts—through pride, envy, anger, laziness, covetousness, gluttony, and lust. Every time I go through the list, I find something I've forgotten, a process of getting true and getting honest.

Those of us who have found some serenity in the fellowship and spirituality of twelve-step groups like AA and Al-Anon also know a practice of self-examination. Step 4 of the Twelve Steps directs us to "make a searching and fearless moral inventory of ourselves." The practice isn't designed to make us feel bad, but to make us honest. Step 4 is a spiritual discipline because "we want to find exactly how, when, and where our natural desires have warped us." The "warp" of misplaced or outsized desires is part of what gets us "out of true."

Often, Step 4 is practiced with another person who can help us see where we wobble. We need someone else to get down to eye level with us. When truing a wheel, the mechanic takes it off the bike and puts it on the truing stand to get a better view. She loosens, then tightens the spokes to get the rim back into a perfect circle. A wheel needs some tension, but not too much in any one spot. Consistent tension through the spokes is what holds the rim in the perfect circle.

As bicycle mechanic and guru Sheldon Brown said, an "out-of-true" wheel "will give a bumpy ride even on a smooth road."

When I'm "out of true," it doesn't matter how smooth the road before me. I'm bringing the unevenness to the road.

Curiously, Brother Lawrence doesn't seem all that interested in the dedicated discipline of self-examination. For him, "All penance and other spiritual practices serve only to bring us into union with God through love. After thinking a great deal about spiritual practices, he found the shorter distance is going straight to this union through the continual practice of love, by doing all things for the love of God." Brother Lawrence *does* think we need to "watch attentively over all movements of the soul, in spiritual matters as well as in the most common ones." For those of us who haven't reached Brother Lawrence's level of spiritual enlightenment and so can't be constantly aware of all movements of our souls, a regular practice of reflection gives us a way to figure out why we're "out of true."

I inherited my second set of wheels, wheels far more glorious than I deserved as a novice cyclist. Not long after Hideki met his untimely demise (a story for Chapter 6), I found myself in need of a new bicycle. Abbi and Erich, another bike friend from the neighborhood, cobbled together a complete bike primarily from used parts that I purchased. But the wheels I inherited after Mark died.

I never actually met Mark. He was the husband of Abbi's friend Carol. Mark died of cancer way too young. As the disease and the treatment drained life from his body, Mark's bicycles began collecting dust in the corner of their basement apartment. He was too sick to ride anything. After Mark died, amid all the other details of suddenly becoming a young widow, Carol had to contend with these bicycles. Mark's mountain bike was a pearl-purple custom Ted Wojcik frame. It was a gorgeous bike, too personal to give away and too valuable as a whole to strip for parts. So Carol decided to save the mountain bike for their daughter, Olivia, though she was only in middle school at the time and far too small to ride her father's bike. The BMX bike Carol sold to raise some money to offset all the medical expenses. And she bequeathed to Abbi a set of Mavic wheels from Mark's commuter bike that would become the wheels for my new bike.

Mark's wheels were expensive, far more expensive than any I would buy on my own. So I felt an obligation to protect this inheritance. At the point where the wheel attaches to the front fork, you have a choice: Do you want an easily removable "quick release" skewer, or do you want one that bolts on? The advantage of the quick release is that it's easier to take the wheel off when you need to transport the bike in the back of a car or on an overhead rack. The disadvantage is that bike thieves have a habit of quick-releasing your wheel and stealing it. One way to foil them is to carry a steel cable with you, to thread through the front wheel and then through your lock. So I chose the cable. It adds a bit more weight to my bag, but I'll shoulder that burden to protect Mark's wheels.

I felt then—and I still feel now—a responsibility to safeguard this inheritance I didn't really deserve. I never met

Mark, but here I was, riding around on his wheels. It felt oddly intimate, like wearing another person's clothes. Where had these wheels taken Mark? Where did they go on his last ride? Did Mark know that would be the last time he would ever feel the power of his own legs carrying him up a hill and the rush of wind in his face as he sped back down? The wheels were in good condition because Mark had taken care of them. Did he know they would be passed on to another person? When you pick up a used book, the side notes or marginalia tell you something about the previous reader. That little nick in the rim—was that from jumping a curb? But besides that nick, there wasn't much to see. The wheels themselves couldn't tell me much about their prior owner and his adventures. Still, I wondered what roads they rolled on.

This is the religious life, riding on wheels you didn't make or purchase but inherited. Sure, you make the bike your own, you customize it to a certain extent, but you also follow patterns and traditions formed by those before you. And doing that requires developing new habits, new intentions, greater discipline—and keeping the wheels working right. You can't just put those inherited wheels on your frame and keep riding forever, because the riding causes wear and tear. The wheels need periodic assessment and adjustment to stay "true." To keep moving, you occasionally need to stop.

Chapter 3

Saddle | Endurance

Get accustomed to suffering. . . . The world does not understand these truths, and that does not surprise me.

Brother Lawrence, letter to
"Reverend and very honored Mother . . ."

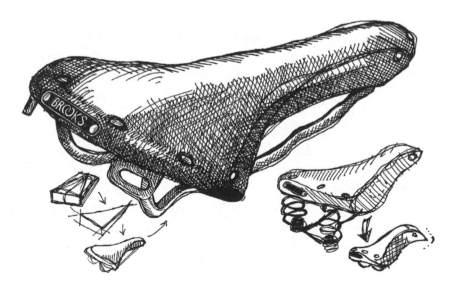

There is spiritual wisdom to be gained by considering a pain in your ass.

It's awkward to talk about, but riding a bicycle regularly prompts a fair amount of thinking about the state of one's butt. Decorum usually suggests that one does not talk about one's derrière, but the embodied life of a cyclist blows past this boundary. Also, hang around cyclists long enough, and eventually the conversation will move southward.

Cyclists are the people who developed padded shorts. We are the people who have developed chamois cream to address the unfortunate truth that skin chafes on a bike saddle. Even a casual cyclist will quickly come to the conclusion that it only takes a few miles in the saddle before their out-of-practice butt hurts. For cyclists, a pain in the butt can be alleviated, but not entirely avoided.

There are three points of contact between the bicycle and the rider: hands and handlebars; feet and pedals; butt and saddle. It's remarkable that a rider can stay upright on a bike with so little contact with the ground. Her hands steer, her feet propel her forward, and her butt, well, it bears the brunt of her weight on the bike. The stronger the cyclist, the more weight can be borne by her core and her legs. Not surprisingly, novice or out-of-practice cyclists often experience more pain in their rears via the saddle.

If you're "in the saddle," your butt also absorbs the bumps of an uneven road. If you've got enough advance warning before encountering curbs or potholes, you can stand up on the pedals, lifting your butt out of the saddle, and aim to absorb the bumps with your bent legs. Strong legs are a form of suspension, with core muscles providing the majority of support. But most of the time as you move along the road, your butt is where the majority of your weight lands on the bike.

What the bicycle evangelists don't tell you about re-learning to ride is that your butt is going to hurt. If you're in the saddle long enough, you develop calluses on your sitz bones (technically, the tuberosity of the ischium, or *tuber ischiadicum* in Latin). This is basically a good thing, because calluses allow you to stay in the saddle longer, but still, it's disconcerting—or at least it was for me. I first noticed the fabric wearing away on the rear of my pants in two small spots. And then in the shower one day, I noticed a slight rough patch on the back of each thigh at the top. At our next meeting, in a hushed voice, I asked the church-lady bike sherpas about it, and they assured me this was all perfectly normal.

Guitar players develop calluses on their fingers; farmers build up rough spots where they hold their tools; painters stain their hands with pigment. I've turned my hands temporarily plum-colored by peeling beets. But a change in such an intimate place threw me. Calluses on your butt are an external reminder of an internal reality—the bike changes you.

A broken-in butt is a sign of initiation into this fellowship of cyclists. You are no longer a casual cyclist; your body has been mortified by the saddle.

Conversations about saddles are prone to anxiety and hyperbole. At the advent of the first cycling boom, the saddle itself was problematic for women. For one thing, a saddle caused them to separate their legs to get their feet on the pedals on either side of a high-wheeler. The "solution" of side-saddle, borrowed from horseback riding, clearly wouldn't work for a bicycle. Early adult tricycles avoided the social anxiety over women's separated legs, and solved the awkward problem women faced in jumping up to mount a high-wheeler.

A saddle also brought up taboo topics. Victorian doctors and critics opined against women cyclists for fear of the possible sexual stimulation from the saddle in contact with genitalia. These same critics also feared that cycling would compromise women's fertility and child-bearing capacity. All of this anxiety about women and saddles was an expression of the cultural fear of and attempt to control women's bodies. But, as Robert Penn points out, "The threat of tens of thousands of permanently aroused nymphomaniacs cruising around the countryside never materialized."

Saddles are personal and intimate, not least because of what they hold up and where they reside. Made of leather, cloth, or plastic, saddles also come in a variety of sizes. The stock saddle sold with most comfort hybrid bikes or beach cruisers is most like a couch cushion—bulky, squishy, and designed to fit every rear that sits upon it. The unfortunate truth? More padding—whether made of gel or lamb's wool—doesn't necessarily make for a more comfortable ride. No amount of padding can get around the fact that one's bum has to come in contact with the saddle in order to support one's weight.

Hideki, my first bike, had an old black-leather saddle—an Avocet—which, oddly enough, seemed to fit almost perfectly without much fiddling. The leather was broken in, and the width seemed just right for me. I love this saddle so much I've since transferred it onto other bikes.

A good-fitting saddle is a thing of beauty. For generations, Brooks saddles have been the gold standard of high craftsmanship and comfort. Made in England, these leather saddles have a cult-like following. Like a pair of good shoes or a baseball glove, the saddle needs to be broken in. Brooks saddles reward your dedication; in a disposable culture, they are an anomalous product that "improves with use." As you ride, over time, the leather molds itself to the contours of your rear. You don't conform to it; the saddle conforms to you. Which makes it easier to stay in the saddle.

Cyclists have made many attempts to diminish the pain of the saddle. Padding is standard for most cycling shorts, which now means that most male cyclists have some idea of what it feels like to walk around with a menstruation pad, circa 1985, in one's underwear. Chamois butter can be applied to one's arse before a long ride, in an attempt to minimize the friction between the rear and the saddle. But the reality is, there's only so much we can do to minimize the suffering of the saddle. Instead, we learn to endure it.

Suffering can be formative. But there's nothing holy about being forced into pain. Religious distortions about "salvific suffering" have been tools of oppression, selectively applied, forcing some to stay down. At the same time, some suffering is unavoidable, and it offers a particular knowledge that seems to come only from getting close to our human fragility. The suffering of the saddle, while inescapable, is freely chosen; we don't have to be in the saddle, but we choose to stay.

Brother Lawrence counsels his correspondent to "get accustomed to suffering." I understand that: I'm familiar with the suffering of being on my bike. When I've been off my bike for a while, my legs feel heavier and my butt is achier. When I'm riding regularly, the pain of being in the saddle sets a familiar baseline, a suffering to which I'm accustomed. In fact, the discipline of staying in the saddle makes it possible to go further and endure more.

We ride further when we ride together. When I go out on my own, I can ride far, but I can go further with someone else. Companions don't eliminate my experience of pain, but they help me realize I'm not experiencing it alone. I'm much more likely to endure the pain of hours in the saddle with another person, especially someone else accustomed to the suffering that I'm feeling.

Staying in the saddle takes intentionality. Cyclists choose this acceptable amount of pain over the ease of a car or a bus. We make the decision to keep our butts in the saddle, to stay put. Some Christian monastic communities also make an intentional decision to stay put. In addition to their vows of poverty, obedience, and chastity, they make "vows of stability." Monks and nuns in the Benedictine tradition pledge stability to a particular community, a particular place, sometimes a city.

A city is, almost by definition, a place of flux. People come and people go, out of choice and out of necessity. During my twenties in Boston, I seemed to move every two years. I didn't really start to feel connected to the city until I lived in one neighborhood for five years. It's hard to build "thick" neighborly relationships when you're moving all the time. To live here responsibly and faithfully invites a vow of stability.

If you look at it closely, the city will break your heart. But you've got to stay in the saddle long enough to see it.

When I cycle through all of Boston, not just the "good" parts where the tourists visit or the bike paths guide, the collective pain of our city becomes visible. Because I've been riding these roads for so long, my eyes have become familiar with my city's grief.

My temptation is to choose the clear paths that avoid the blatant displays of suffering. My temptation is to take another route to avoid seeing the same man, already drunk by ten A.M., who sits with his backpack and his dirty toupee on the same street corner every day.

By bike, I'm learning to resist my temptation and become more deeply acquainted with my city's suffering, slowing down enough to see all the small crucifixions on street corners. Lampposts become memorials to the city's dead, with offerings of teddy bears and candles and liquor bottles.

Roadside memorials fade exponentially from the first day they're erected. Teddy bears don't weather well in Boston snow. Grief gets dirtier and more embarrassing, until the offerings to the dead are cleaned up and cleared out late some night.

By bike, it's easier to see the public pain. Foreclosed homes shutter their former occupants' dreams inside until they're bulldozed into the ground. Empty lots bear the claw-marks of bulldozers so that not even empty houses stand in memorial. Photocopied posters of lost dogs and lost humans fade as the winter wind slowly peels away layers of ink and memory.

Even by bike, what is harder to see is the hidden suffering: the invisible damage done to every child in the neighborhood who has learned to recognize the sound of gunshots by the age of three. What is harder to see is the hidden trauma of the sanitation workers who are unwittingly tasked as shrine undertakers, dismantling the decaying roadside memorials late at night. How do we learn to see the hidden suffering of the EMTs who have revived the same addict seven or eight times, and then never see her again? How do we learn to see the hidden suffering of that addict, who has been scuttled away to a shelter on an uninhabited street?

We stay in the saddle.

We stay in the saddle. We become accustomed to the suffering, to build up some wherewithal to keep looking, but not so accustomed that we no longer see. We build up capacity to see the pain, but are not so blinded by it that we can't keep moving.

To get acquainted with the grief of this city, I've biked it for a long time—for so long now that I see ghosts, ghosts of ghost bikes, those stark white bikes that mark the places where cyclists have been severely injured or killed.

This is the spiritual discipline of the bike: Look. Stay. Do not look away. Do not take a different route. Do not cross to the other side of the road. Accompany your neighbors in their suffering. See as you wish to be seen. This is the urban spiritual discipline of seeing.

A constitutive mark of a city is transience—at least that's what some urban theorists insist. And Boston is a mixed city of the permanent and the transient. No wonder it's taken me over a decade here to feel permanent. The possibility of leaving was always on the horizon, even for me. I never thought I'd stay, since the dominant narratives of both my generation and my city told a story of people who cycle through and leave.

Amid all the flux and flow of life, the people who stay make a commitment to a particular piece of earth, to a particular city.

It took time for me to commit to my city. Ten years ago, I considered signing up to be a Big Sister, but they required a three-year commitment, and I never thought I'd stay here that long. I didn't make an intentional decision to be here until more recently. My vow to Boston built up slowly over time, a patina of the grit of the city.

This city may not be the world's best-tailored saddle designed perfectly for me. But it is broken in, and it does fit. Despite all the bumps of Boston that drive me crazy—the parochialism that red-shirts newcomers for not just years but generations, the Yankee independence, the icy personal affect, the widening income divide that keeps the poor from ever thriving—this is the city that I have formed to, and it has formed to me. I am learning to stay in this particular saddle.

Chapter 4

Tires and Tubes | Border-Crossing

He called the practice of the presence of God the shortest and easiest road to Christian perfection, the very form and life of virtue, and the great protection against sin. He assured his friends that to make this practice easier and to form the habit of it in ourselves, we only need courage and willingness, and he proved this truth even better by his deeds than by his words. For it was seen, when he did his duty as a cook, that in the midst of an arduous task, even in the midst of the most attention-diverting duties, his mind and spirit were fixed on God.

from Brother Lawrence's Eulogy by the Abbé of Beaufort

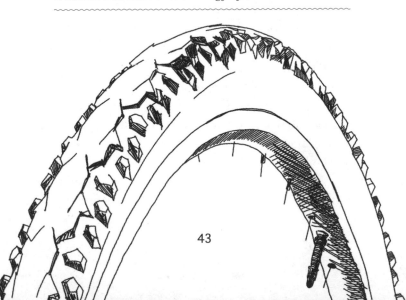

There was blood on my tires.

The "shortest and easiest road" home that night took me along the bike path.

Next to the police officer was a young boy, standing hunched with a rag to his chin, blood on the pavement below. None of the people standing there saw me coming. When I awkwardly rang my bell, the cluster of men stepped off the bike path to allow me to pass, but there wasn't sufficient space for me to cycle past without riding through that small, child-sized puddle of blood.

Even at dusk, I saw the stain on my front tire. With every rotation, my tire landed on the pavement, stamping an imprint. I didn't cause the bloodstain, but on my tires I carried it.

Tires have a repeating pattern, a set of groves and ridges to channel water away. Over and over again, those patterns marked the pavement with blood as I rode, until all that was left was the stain on my tires.

I don't know what happened back there on the bike path, under the street light.

As I rode home, I wondered if I should have done something differently. I had recently affixed a "Clergy" license plate to my bike rack, mostly as a joke after my ordination as a pastor, since I no longer had a car. Should I have stopped, or would that have just been a distraction? The young man, standing a foot shorter than all those tall men in uniforms encircling him—would it have helped him to have a pastor there? What would I have said? How could I be a chaplain to my city if I was too anxious to stop?

Around and around my stained tires went, while a private tragedy in a public space moved further and further into the distance behind me.

I checked Twitter and the police blotter when I got home, but there was no report from the bike path. Those of us dedicated to the city, its people and its streets—we are observers of stories half-told, painful, and unresolved in public places. The shortest and easiest road can be damn hard some nights.

The next morning, on the way to my office, I took the bike path. There was no sign of the previous night, except a small, dark spot on the pavement. I stopped. Had the young boy been mugged? Beaten up? Did some other kids take his bike? Nothing in that place answered my questions or assuaged my own lingering guilt that I could have done more to be a better neighbor, a better pastor to that boy and my city.

The morning bike traffic kept passing me by. There was no more information to be gained from looking at this stain on the ground. So finally I got back on my bike and rode into downtown. At the end of the day, I rode back to my neighborhood, then to the grocery store, and finally home, but my tires continued to wear the scene of the previous night.

Every street I've traveled is recorded on my tires. The road debris gets caught in the tires' grooves, a microscopic history of where I've been: grass from when I jumped off the bike path to avoid hitting a small dog off-leash, gum from the road where the construction workers tear down and build up near Dudley Square, a splash of coffee from the spilled cup of Dunkin' Donuts that a motorist left on top of their car and drove away with, and a pungent mix of mud and goose poop from the Muddy River breaching its banks onto the bike path. All evidence of the remarkable and the mundane, recorded on my tires.

Bicycle tires and wheels are crucial to the utility and practicality of a bicycle. Walking can move us, but wheels move us faster. With solid rubber and no inflation, the earliest iterations of bicycle tires were unforgiving and heavy. The modern bicycle would never have found its popularity were it not for innovations in tires and tubes. The invention of pneumatic tires allowed the modern safety bicycle to be lighter and absorb more instability on the emerging network of American roads. Modern bicycle tires are actually made up of two key parts: the outside casing of thick rubber and the interior inflatable tube. The inflated tube presses on the tire. Imagine if you were just riding on the tube: every time that tube punctured, you'd have a flat. But with the heavier rubber encasing the inflated tube, you can roll over uneven surfaces without constantly "flatting."

Bike tubes require regular inflation because they lose a bit of pressure whether they're ridden or not. Each tire has a recommended range of inflation. Over-inflation transfers all of the bumps in the road to the cyclist's body. Under-inflation causes the bike to drag. Cyclists aim for just the right amount of pressure.

No matter how heavy the tire casing is, flats and punctures are unavoidable. Despite what the bike industry tries to sell, there's no such thing as a puncture-proof tire. Shattered glass, sharp rocks, or an upturned nail will always get through. And no tire lasts forever. Even sequestering a bike won't preserve its tires. Eventually, a bike that stays in a basement for years will have flat tires because of the inevitable leaking of air over time.

The bottom line is that no amount of tire maintenance will protect us. The best we can do is be prepared with a patch kit, a spare tube, or someone to call to help us out. At some point, some misery will come our way. Our tires will go flat just when we're running late and rushing to an important event, and we'll be dropped to our knees by the side of the road to attend to our brokenness.

The bicycle sherpas who taught me how to ride also taught me how to fix a flat. In most places in the city, I'm not too far from a bike shop where I can pay someone to fix a flat for me. But self-repair is cheaper, and the bike sherpas also convinced me that I would, in fact, flat at an inconvenient time, so I should learn to fix it myself. We watched a ton of YouTube videos, but mostly we practiced taking off the tire and tube and putting them back on.

And the sherpas were right. The first time I flatted while bike commuting, I was on my way to an important meeting. I rolled in late and slightly out of breath, my bright red manicure scuffed with black smudges from the tires, but I had the distinct glow of someone who can fix her own problem. I know it's a minor accomplishment, but for me and for the many women I suspect were steered away from mechanical skills when they were growing up, repairing our own machines is thrilling. And my skills have grown. Now I can stop along the bike path and help a stranded cyclist put in a new tube. Flats have become simply a part of riding.

Tires come in a wide range of colors and treads, from slick to deeply grooved. Mountain bike tires are covered in knobs of rubber to roll over rocks and loose dirt. Road bike tires have barely any texture at all. Cyclo-cross and commuter tires fall somewhere in between. My commuter bike, affectionately known as "ClergyBike" in honor of that license plate, boasts wider, grooved tires. My single-speed, affectionately known as "Incognito," rides with smooth road tires. It's not very good for rain or grit, but wicked fast on a clean road. But for those of us who are four-season practical cyclists, a change in the weather sometimes prompts a change in tires. It's how we adapt.

For those who follow the ancient practice of keeping the Christian liturgical calendar, that sense of changing and preparing to meet a new season seems oddly familiar. Each season, on the bike and off, has a different emphasis. Winter tires are a preventative strike against the coming snow and icy roads. I switch to winter tires just around the time Advent comes, often waiting for that first snowfall. Thick, knobby winter tires can get you through, but they're heavy, and their textured surface drags on the pavement. Some cyclists even switch to studded tires during the winter—tires with tiny metal knobs on the surface to increase the grip of the tire on icy roads.

I try to switch out of winter tires as soon as I can. Lent, which provides a wide stretch of time for self-reflection, always seems perfectly timed for the snow melt, which reveals the green of new growth. This early taste of spring prompts a celebratory change of tires, a bit thinner and lighter than the winter tires. By the time Eastertide arrives—a great big old party of life triumphing over death—I'm itching to move more freely outside.

Each season requires some adjustments in thought and in practice. Tires ask you to know the conditions in which you ride.

As the point of contact with the ground, tires also ask you to know the quality of the roads on which you travel. All roads have a distinct terrain—dirt or gravel, paved or cobblestoned. Most general-purpose tires can handle these variances. As I've biked Boston's varied roads, I've observed two things about our streets. First, at any given point, about half our roads will be under construction, complicating an already confusing web of streets and often without the promise that the repaired roads will be any safer for cyclists. Second, no road is neutral—all roads are political.

Cyclists are particularly aware of this. As we ride, we notice which roads get plowed first, paved first, repaired first. Roads have biases. Roads have a history of people and policies, neighborhoods built or displaced. Rolling the tires over these roads in each season is a decision about where we move and how we move and what we'll see. And those of us who move to a city, who adopt a city, who make a vow of stability to a city—we have an obligation to learn the history of these roads. To commit to a city means to inherit these roads and all that comes with them. As my tires roll over the "shortest and easiest" roads, I try to remember that the building of them may have meant that their neighborhoods were systemically and historically violated in the process. To cross these neighborhood borders asks me to remember that what is now a direct and smooth path for me may have been quite bumpy for generations before me.

The end of Southwest Corridor, the bike path I take most days, dumps me onto Columbus Avenue for the last mile of my route. The road here is thick with history. Boston was the American home of the modern bicycle frame: Pope Manufacturing Company started in Boston in 1876. Pope Manufacturing eventually became Columbia Bicycles and moved to Westfield, Massachusetts. Now the Pope building on Columbus Avenue is home to luxury condos and a very fancy restaurant.

After about four years of riding the Southwest Corridor every day, I migrated off this protected path. Because the path is physically separated from cars, it feels safe. But a monotony had set in. Along the edges of the bike path are cars and trees, but no neighborhoods. My vow of stability felt boring. So I turned to another route: the "unprotected" Washington Street. Equally as direct as the Corridor path, Washington Street shoots through the city, from my Jamaica Plain neighborhood through Egleston Square, then through Roxbury into Dudley Square, cutting through the South End, then through

Bay Village and Chinatown, and finally into Downtown Crossing, where I turn to climb up Beacon Hill.

Washington is just one street, but it tethers together so many distinct neighborhoods. Biking through the neighborhoods at eye level, I continue to see things once hidden from me on the subway, in the car, and even on the bike path. As I bike through Egleston Square in the morning, the bodega owners sweep the front steps. As the road runs through Chinatown, if I'm biking before nine A.M., I catch the delivery trucks dropping off whole tunas to the Thousand Chef Trading Company, fish so big it takes one man at the head and one at the tail to offload them. One night in the summertime, my bike now rolling on slick tires, I went home along Washington Street after dark, when the air had finally cooled enough so that I could move again. I could hear them before I could see them. Slowing down, I took a good look. Just behind a wooden fence, with a string of bare bulbs lighting up their faces, were two people salsa dancing. They must have been eighty years old! Riding through these neighborhoods, on these tires and through these seasons, I meet a secret Boston.

In certain places Washington Street has "sharrows," those painted lines on the pavement, stylized arrows meant to remind motorists to "share the road" with cyclists. But painted lines don't stop cars from double-parking or swerving into your lane. The lane on Washington is dedicated for buses and bicycles, and while we mostly co-exist, at the end of the day, we cyclists know that the bus is fifty times our size and can do far more damage to us than we can do to it. For now, the tradeoff is worth it—a little more activity in my path for a better view of the city.

I do sometimes miss the Southwest Corridor. Most mornings I would cross paths with a gaggle of nursery school children holding on to a rope as their teachers led them down the Corridor from their school to the park. Nothing makes you feel more like a superhero than ringing your bike bell repeatedly and waving furiously to four-year-olds who shout with glee back to you. I don't see them when I ride on Washington Street. But here I see more adults starting their days. I hear far more languages spoken. And I see lots of kids getting on school buses—an ever-present reminder of Boston's school-busing history, a long and complicated saga of our racially segregated neighborhoods and desegregation efforts through mandated busing.

I'm convinced that intentional border-crossing is an essential practice of urban spirituality. Border-crossing requires both great grace and a high threshold for awkwardness as we bump into one another and our inherited histories. We cannot live well together in a city without learning how to cross man-made borders, carefully and gently.

One work trip took me to Charleston, South Carolina, where I was stuck without a bicycle. Charleston doesn't have a bike-share program, and I've not yet caved to purchasing a folding bike for business travel. Still, exploring a new city on foot is my kind of heaven, and I discovered that Charleston felt complicated. The main commercial street seemed like a white fantasia. The only people of color present on the street were those employed by the stores and restaurants. I wandered to The Old Slave Mart Museum, where a volunteer guided me through the building once used as a slave auction gallery. Once there were many structures here for the sale of enslaved people; now the gallery is the only one still standing. After the inside tour, the guide led me behind the museum, and we stood on newly paved asphalt, yellow lines marking the spots for cars where a century before there had been temporary housing for those sold into slavery. Sometimes the borders you cross are hidden. Unless someone had guided me, I would never have known that the pavement beneath my feet in that parking lot was stained with blood.

But biking through Boston later that year, I saw how my city had paved over our own history. On an unremarkable Monday morning in September, after I had switched over to my Washington Street route and pulled up to the light at Egleston Square, I noticed red pigment on my tires. Looking back along the road behind me, I saw a faded red line curve along the sidewalk and onto the road, a red line that wove along the street beyond my line of sight. The red dust gathered in the channels of my tires, sticking to the rubber treads. When the light changed from red to green, I was carried off by the traffic to my left, my tires again stamping the ground with red dust.

It was only when I got into my office and searched the Internet that I discovered my tires had rolled in an intentional mix of crushed brick and red pigment. The bricks were acquired from demolished buildings in our neighborhood and then mixed with red chalk. Two days before, activists and artists from City Life/Vida Urbana had taken the carts used to lay down the lines on baseball fields and recreated the "red-line" demarcation once used to exclude communities of color from federal housing loans. I had rolled in it. And I do roll in it.

When we roll through neighborhoods and cross borders, our tires record the journey: blood, dust, mud. We always ride with something stuck to our tires. We live with these histories. The challenge to border-crossers and those who value a kind of spiritual attentiveness to the city is to tread lightly. When I look at the 1936 Federal Housing Administration map, my house is within the borders of the red-lined area. My neighborhood is now known for its racial diversity; that's one of the reasons I moved here ten years ago. And yet, my home was likely once owned by a black family at some point, probably one among the many systematically denied loans because of red-lining. The red dust I roll through reminds me that Boston's racial history isn't far beneath the surface of our roads.

The miracle of bicycles is that you can ride anywhere. You can just go. You don't need to wait for a road to be built, or a bus to come, or enough gas in your tank, or enough money for a taxi. You just go. But it would be naïve to think that my riding across the red-lines somehow restores my city or rights something within myself. There's still a blood stain on my tires, even if I didn't personally cause it. If we're disciplined enough—and, as Brother Lawrence would say, attentive and humble enough—to look for it, we'll see the still-visible stain of our history. Tire treads repeat, again and again.

Cities make visible certain things we'd rather not see. Our vulnerability and frailty and poverty and violence are public. If I take my bike on the Southwest Corridor on a Thursday, along Columbus Street I'll run into the women pushing their grocery carts in the wrong direction in the bike lane. Their carts are full of beer bottles they've sorted out of the recycling bins outside the college housing along Columbus Street. They gather these bottles out of necessity, despite the public shame of digging in other people's garbage. For every bottle they scavenge, they get just five cents. Their hard labor and fragile existence are clearly visible in the city.

In Eastern Christianity, there's a deep spiritual practice of using icons, holy objects, and images as means for prayer and meditation. To pray with icons is to gaze on the visible and to see what is invisible. You look at an icon, observing all you can, wondering about figures in the image, imagining their stories, drifting into a conversation with them. You gaze upon the light around the saint's halo, wondering where it comes from. Your sight softens around the edges. The icon is the thing you look through to see something far deeper: the face of God.

It was Brother Lawrence who taught me to pray in the city. He seemed capable of turning anything into an icon—the pots he washed, the potatoes he was peeling, whatever was in front of him to do and observe. When the Abbé of Beaufort eulogized Brother Lawrence, he said, "For it was seen, when he did his duty as a cook, that in the midst of an arduous task, even in the midst of the most attention-diverting duties, his mind and spirit were fixed on God." In Brother Lawrence's practice of being in the presence of God, everything can be an icon.

When I ride my bike, the road in front of me is my meditative object. My sight softens around the edges. As I ride, I can still see the road, but in the repetition of the tires rolling over the pavement again and again, I quiet my mind and look through. The road becomes the icon, blood-stained and redlined, with all the humanity of the children walking to school and the workers delivering fish and the women pushing their carts of beer bottles. The road becomes the icon of this broken and holy city.

Chapter 5

Lights | Visibility

The goal of all his [Brother Lawrence's] actions was to do
them for the love of God. He found great satisfaction in
doing this. He was even contented to pick up one single
straw from the ground for the love of God. He looked for
God alone and nothing else, not even [God's] gifts.

The Abbé of Beaufort on Conversation with
Brother Lawrence, September 8, 1666

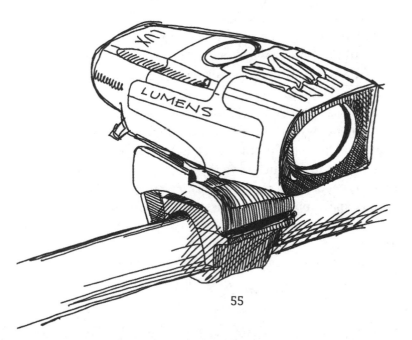

"Hey!" I shout, as the car drifts into the bike lane. "I didn't see you!" the driver shouts back through his closed window.

"I'm right here!" I shout again.

"F—— you!" he yells.

This is almost a daily conversation on the road, a call and response, if I get the courtesy of a response. The rhythm is the same: I shout whatever first comes to mind, and keep it short, clipped, and loud. "Hey!" "Yo!" "Stop!" "Watch out" is a good one, but two syllables can take too much time. Some days I'm doing the swearing. Some days there is no response. Rarely do I hear, "I'm sorry."

No doubt, the roads in Boston have become much more bicycle-friendly in the years I've been riding here, but still, each day is a fight to stay visible and safe.

Every exchange with a driver offers an opportunity to show love and generally not be a jerk. To meet the ignorance or obliviousness of my neighbor with gentleness, clarity, and grace is a spiritual discipline. My aim is to be unfailingly polite when I ride, though it's hard to keep this ethic when someone is careening into me at forty-five miles an hour.

Just to be clear: I'm not a perfect cyclist. I've failed to see what's in front of me in ways that endangered the safety of others. A thousand times I've cut short a pedestrian popping out from between parked cars. True, they shouldn't be crossing where there's no crosswalk, but between a bike and a pedestrian, a bicycle can do greater damage and so bears the greater responsibility. I try to hold to the ethic that "an enlightened commuter defers to the more vulnerable party." I believe in proportional responsibility on our roads: the more dangerous one's vehicle, the more responsibility one has to be careful. Or, as Bike Snob (Eben Weiss) puts it, "Cars kill, whereas bicycles mostly just annoy."

Driving a car gives me a greater illusion of safety. On my

bike, I know that I'm vulnerable. The lack of a giant metal shell around me makes it clear that my safety and survival depend on both my own care in riding and my visibility to others.

Riding a bicycle on the regular requires the cyclist to be visible. I'll get run over if I'm not seen, so my very life depends on my visibility. This isn't ego or entitlement, but a simple fact: If I'm not visible, I'm not safe. A mature urban spirituality asks us to commit to daily practices—including border-crossings and vows of stability—so that we might truly see the city to which we've committed ourselves. Bike commuting has taught me the inverse spiritual practice of making myself visible.

Riding anywhere requires an intentional practice of making one's self visible. Cars are a factor in country riding, but without the frequency of the city. In true country cycling, you can go for miles without encountering a car. Once a horse and buggy tailed my buddy Erich while he was riding among the Amish in Yates County, New York. Riding in the sparsely populated Vermont hills, I've seen more cows than cars. Still, careful cycling is critical.

I find riding in the suburbs more stressful than city riding. While the roads are often wider, the drivers in the suburbs aren't looking for you. Bikes in the burbs are considered either toys for children or weekend recreation for adults, not vehicles of transportation or utility as they are in the city. At least in the city, we've started to condition drivers to keep an eye out for cyclists.

Lights are a primary tool for visibility. Technically they're not part of the bicycle; they're what most dealers call an "after-purchase add-on." In Massachusetts, both front and rear lights are required for night riding. Most cyclists ride with a blinking white light in the front and a blinking red light in the back.

The cruel truth is simple: I can make myself highly visible and still get hit. I've made several modifications to my bike and gear in order to become more visible: I've put lights all over my frame, reflective tape on my jacket, even had my frame powder-coated in retroreflective paint. (When I started riding regularly, my mother sent me a construction worker's yellow vest, but it's really too ridiculous to wear in public.) Across the city, you see bikes with homemade hack-jobs to increase visibility, giving their riders every good chance to be seen and be safe. However we outfit our rides, we're all just trying to get seen.

Urban cyclists learn to ride presuming we are *unseen.* Danger comes in the driver who's racing through the yellow light and cuts you off from the other direction, or the driver who might "right hook" you, oblivious to the cyclist on their right side as they make a right turn. The distracted driver is an especially dangerous breed. Distracted drivers aren't dependable, and they don't see everything around them. Cyclists learn to look for the telltale signs of preoccupied drivers. They keep turning their eyes from the road to their laps or their hands. We see their heads dip down and then jerk back up. As we ride at eye level, we can see into the car windows, see the secret lives of drivers—eating sandwiches, painting fingernails, wrapping a present at a stoplight, talking on their phones. The phone is the worst, as I know from personal experience.

Waiting at an intersection to make a turn onto a busy road, I noticed the car next to me drifting into my bike lane. The driver's eyes were cast down, his hands on his phone and the steering wheel balanced between his knees. "Hey!" I shouted, though with the radio and air conditioning on, and his earphones in, he didn't seem to hear me. The car drifted slowly closer, the driver's eyes still down and the light still red. If he hit the gas at this angle, he'd drive directly into me. At this point he was so close to me that I could reach out and touch his passenger window—so I did. Putting a hand flat on the glass, I shouted, "I can see you texting," which in retrospect may not have been the most spiritually mature opening line. He jerked his head up, confused, and turned the wheel back left. "F—— you!" he shouted back. The light turned green and he was gone.

We all have friends and loved ones who move through life distracted, unaware of how their stopping and swerving are throwing off the people around them. In the city, with so many people living in such a small space, we're bound to be impacted by one another's distracted movements. I've had fellow Bostonians walk right into me on the sidewalk, their eyes not on their path but on their phones. But sometimes I'm the distracted one, unaware of how my movements are impacting others.

On the road with my bicycle, the conditions are unpredictable enough that I won't try to multitask. As a cyclist, I aim for dependability—ride in a straight line, don't swerve in and out, and stop at stoplights. My increased visibility and dependability help, but in the end, I'm dependent on others seeing me.

During my years of riding daily in Boston, I've been hit twice. The first time the driver was going too fast around a blind curve and didn't see me. The second time was a classic bicycle collision known as "getting doored." Biking the final leg of my office commute, I was rolling down Washington Street as it becomes a single one-way street. I moved to the center of the lane just as a taxi cab pulled towards the curb on the left—and a tourist opened the passenger-side door into oncoming traffic, including me. I was going slowly enough to panic-brake and escape with only a door-shaped bruise on my left thigh. The tourist just didn't look before she opened her door—a minor oversight that could have had far worse consequences. This kind of accident teaches us that our obliviousness or distractedness can hurt other people.

The daily discipline of riding and thinking about my visibility has slowly shaped my self-perception: I am worth being seen.

The spirituality of twelve-step fellowships offers the idea that spiritual maturity is about getting "right-sized," not so big that we overwhelm the people around us and not so small that we disappear. Sometimes the road feels like an arms race of cars getting bigger and bigger as motorists buy into the mythology that size will save them. Bike Snob mockingly traces this trend back to biblical times: "God's instructions to Noah were basically the world's first car commercial and the sales pitch was this: Large vehicles are your salvation." The city is full of SUVs driven by people who have never been off-road a day in their lives and who try to parallel park in compact spaces. I've ridden my bike behind a Hummer down an old Boston one-way alley, the car so large that I couldn't see around either side. When Dr. Anita Kurmann was killed riding her bike in Boston, the cycling community wondered what on earth a massive eighteen-wheeler was doing driving down Massachusetts Avenue, a tight, congested city street. As cyclists, our visibility is at least partially dependent on not being in the shadow of others.

As more and more urban residents turn to bicycles for

cheap, dependable, efficient transportation, only some of those cyclists are publicly visible. Cycling advocacy groups speak of "invisible cyclists": those who can't come to infrastructure meetings, don't fill out online surveys, aren't connected to neighborhood bicycle groups. Often the "invisible cyclists" are literally invisible, riding without lights on whatever bikes they have access to. Cycling innovators like Noah and Jovanny De Amor are creating "bicycle kitchens," co-educational spaces like Boston's Bowdoin Bike School, designed to reach young people and cyclists unseen and underserved by other bike shops.

The invisible cyclists are on the road, if you have eyes to see. When I ride at off-peak hours, late at night when the restaurants are closing, I see the invisible cyclists forced to use bikes for transit since the subway has shut down for the night. If I ride before dawn, I see the invisible cyclists who have retro-fitted their bikes with grocery carts and wagons trailing behind, filled with the tin cans and beer bottles picked out of other people's recycling bins. These cyclists don't turn up at "Bike to Work Day," though every day they bike to work. And they will remain invisible unless we choose to see them as fellow cyclists.

Visibility or invisibility can be taught. As a woman growing up in this culture, I've been shaped by cultural norms that taught me to be inoffensive. I've learned to hunch my shoulders, to make my body compact. Watch how women and men sit on the subway or public benches, and you'll see immediately the different ways that men are acculturated to take up space, spreading their legs wide, while women have learned to cross their legs and make themselves small.

My bike has given me a certain self-confidence as I ride.

My legs are strong enough to get me where I want to go; I can find a route through unfamiliar places; I am worth being seen. And the longer I ride, the clearer I've become: my life depends on my visibility. But visibility is not as simple as lights and reflective paint.

Some kinds of visibility protect. I don't get profiled for riding what looks like a stolen bike. I don't get pulled over as a possible suspect. And that's because my visibility as a white person affords me unearned protection on the road. Riding home from Dorchester one night from a forum on community relations with the local police, I felt good on my bike as I stretched my legs after spending three tense hours in a steamy church basement, sitting on the edge of a metal chair. I remember picking up speed on the downhill as I cut through Franklin Park, thinking to myself how great it felt to have the wind in my face and to leave the earlier conversation behind. I sped past a police car, hidden in the shadows, and knew I wouldn't be stopped. Knowing that gave me a lurching, sickening sense of my entitlement: my whiteness allows me to presume I can ride through this park undisturbed. I slowed, turning into the traffic circle, making sure the cars saw me before I rode on.

Still, visibility cuts both ways. I need to be visible, and yet my visibility is a problem when those public spaces are hostile—specifically, hostile to me as a woman. Hostile spaces are quick to remind you that your body is not wanted there. Before I commuted by bike, I'd ride the subway regularly. On occasion, I'd be heckled on the train, cat-called or whistled at. But nothing compared to the shouts I get on my bike. I've been hollered at in the middle of a January blizzard when my entire body was covered from my ankles to my eyeballs. I've been called "baby girl" while wearing a long black skirt and black clerical shirt with the white collar, an outfit intentionally designed to be the least sexy clothing possible. The clothing or the context doesn't matter: some visible bodies are problematic in public spaces.

On a recent Sunday night, I returned my Zipcar carshare to its parking spot at the nearby subway station, a place I've walked home from a thousand times. I've learned to keep my keys out and my eyes open. I saw a man walking on the other side of the chain-link fence that separated us. Making eye contact, I nodded hello. Immediately he turned around and started walking towards the place where the fence ended. As he came towards me, he calmly said, "I'm going to throw you in the bushes right there and rape you." A small cluster of bushes were right behind me. Fortunately, the light changed, and I ran across the street into the subway station, physically safe but rattled. He was so calm, so precise.

The next day I went to our neighborhood police station. The guy at the front desk barely raised his head to address me as I retold the story. As I biked back home, a man stuck his head out his truck window and shouted, "I'd like to have your legs wrapped around me too, baby!" "F—— you!" I shouted back, but he was gone. I managed to get home, rage fueling my ride, before bursting into tears. I couldn't even ride the mile and a half home from the police department to report a threat of assault without some jerk commenting on my body.

Some days are quiet, days when I can ride and ring my bell at small children and wave to my neighbors and smile at other cyclists. And some days the quiet of the road is interrupted by someone acting out. It's an act of defiance to put my body into a sometimes-hostile space. I have to believe that having more women and people of color on bikes in public spaces will change the space—maybe not immediately, but soon. And I also know that, although they weren't designed for me, I'm allowed to be on these roads too.

On those quiet days, the road lulls me into contemplation, and then, unannounced, someone breaks in. Drivers who shout unprovoked comments are anonymous Internet trolls made manifest. Most days, I know enough to ignore their stupidity. I am thrown off less by the content of their shouts than by the interruption of my ride.

The city demands of cyclists that we see and get seen, that we keep our eyes fixed and searching. The Abbé of Beaufort observed that Brother Lawrence "looked for God alone and nothing else." His eyes were fixed. Brother Lawrence imagined a world shot through with the possibility that God was in all things, if he had eyes to see it. He presumed that there was something holy to be seen everywhere, if we have eyes to see it. We put lights on our bikes to help others see us, but also to help us see what's really in front of us, to make sure we're seeing clearly. Riding in the dark, we use lights to ensure we don't mistake a pothole for an oil slick, or a shadow for a pothole. Cycling through the city demands that we see what is really before us so we don't hurt ourselves or our neighbors.

On the quiet days, uninterrupted by horns or hecklers, I've observed the makeshift monuments to hurt and heartache on our city streets. At the corner of Washington Street and Columbus Avenue was a roadside shrine following the death of Brianna Bigby, age twenty-three, shot in June 2013 while sitting in a car nearby. The lamppost memorial grew daily with candles, teddy bears, and balloons. As the weeks went by, the balloons deflated. The ink ran off the signs, leaving blank white poster-board lashed to the lamppost. As I biked past each day that summer, the objects slowly curdled into clumps at the base of the pole. Then one day the whole thing was gone.

This isn't the only roadside shrine I've passed, but the

memorials are concentrated in the primarily black and Hispanic neighborhoods. If I bike home from work early, when the kids are being released from the high school near my house, almost every one among the throng of students I see seems to have a button on their jacket memorializing a friend who's been killed. In the suburbs of my childhood, our grief was quarantined to cemeteries or respectable plaques on park benches. In the city, our wounds are more visible, more raw, less respectable. Maybe in the city, we need our suffering to be seen by our neighbors, by God.

The cycling community has its own ritual of visibility and grief: the ghost bike. Chained to a tree or a lamppost near the location where a cyclist was killed, the white-painted ghost bike is a visible sign of a life lost, a dangerous intersection, and the need to be seen. Begun in St. Louis in 2003, the grassroots effort to install ghost bikes has spread across the world. In the beginning, ghost bikes were part of a guerilla tactic; they stayed visible only until some city official took them down. More recently, at least here in Boston, the cyclists have coordinated with the city to identify safe and secure locations for the memorials.

Ever since I started riding regularly, ghost bikes have marked our city, statues to the truth that even as more people ride, more people are getting killed on our roads. Cyclists feel a certain kinship with one another, a dedicated minority who have chosen to pattern their lives with a practice that cuts against the grain. Ghost bikes are signs of our own vulnerability and mortality. *That could have been me*, we think as we ride past. The ghost bike for Kanako Miura, a thirty-six-year-old MIT researcher from Japan killed at Charlesgate West, seems like a caution to all who would ride Beacon Street or Commonwealth Avenue into Kenmore Square, a notorious knot of intersections: "Be ye warned, all who enter here."

In the past, it seemed like ghost bikes would pop up overnight, the work of the underground guild of mourners unknown to those who would pass by. As the cycling community has grown and matured, the act of creating and installing ghost bikes has become more standardized and more visible. Creating ghost bikes is to cyclists what making Jell-O salads is to church ladies: rituals of grief for the good of the community. As observant Jews gather to "sit shiva," observant cyclists gather to mourn at the location of death marked by the ghost bike.

◎═◎▨◎═◎

In the last few years, I've participated in multiple ghost bike dedications, each with a shared grim rhythm, each as particular as the cyclist killed. Through social media, an informal group has emerged to prepare the ghost bike and the dedication ceremony. This group includes those who find a bike, strip it, paint it white, carve a plaque, scout a location, prepare a service, invite the community, transport the bike to the memorial site, and coordinate with the police. Informally, we have become the ghost bike funeral guild.

Marcia Deihl, sixty-five, seemed impossibly, perfectly Cambridge: a folk singer of the feminist old guard who founded the first bisexual solidarity group in Boston and for decades rode her bike across the city. She was killed biking near a grocery store when a dump truck hit her.

I arrived at Marcia's ghost bike dedication thinking that I was just offering a prayer, but discovered there was no order of service. I had officiated at funerals before, but never a ghost bike dedication. And none of my prayer books have instructions on how to bless a ghost bike. Standing in the snow, a few of us huddled under an awning and quickly put something together as waiting mourners began to mill around the nearby lamppost.

At each ghost bike dedication, cyclists show up who have never met the deceased. At Marcia's ghost bike dedication, women from Marcia's consciousness-raising feminist collective stood next to bike messengers, who stood next to members of her Baptist church choir. The longer I've been a part of Boston's cycling community, the more I feel a kinship based not on shared belief, but on shared practice. We all ride. Or as my friend John Adams says, "If they ride a bike, they are bike family. We mourn the loss of a member of our family." I think we cyclists come to these memorials of people we don't know because we share a sense that we too could be in their place. We share a "Rule of Life" to move by bike in a largely hostile environment that shapes both our movements and our sense of mortality. When we gather, we honor a single lost life, as well as a community that is simultaneously bound together, interdependent, and fragile.

We held Marcia's ghost bike dedication in the bitter cold of March. I took my gloves off to turn the pages of my notebook, my fingers turning from pink to white in the cold. We pressed in tightly together to keep warm, standing three rows deep around the bike. The cyclists stamped their feet against the snow, like horses impatient to get moving again. Marcia's friends sang an old protest song. In the strong wind we passed out the candles, unable to light them.

The white ghost bike looked naked in the snow as we left it behind.

By the time I biked home that night, my social networks were ablaze with photos of candles. Cyclist after cyclist had posted a photo of those unlit candles from Marcia's ceremony, now lit in their own homes. With no explicit directions, they had created their own ritual and sign of visibility.

Marcia's ghost bike was a lady's cruiser, with a basket of flowers on the front. For Fritz Philogene, eighteen, we needed a young man's ghost bike, sleek and fast. Fritz, a high-school sophomore who had just earned his first paycheck, was killed in a hit-and-run. The ghost bike guild that had come into formation following Marcia's death sprang into action again for Fritz as we planned the Dorchester dedication.

I admit it: I screwed up Fritz's ghost bike dedication bigtime. We actually dedicated Fritz's ghost bike twice, once and then again as his high school friends got to the right location. The ceremony was way too long and too formal. The attempt to sing together fell flat. Some of Fritz's family members only spoke Haitian Creole, and the service was all in English. I misread the cultural context, not realizing that the template that had worked for Marcia's service wouldn't work for Fritz's. I was careless with my fellow cyclist Noah, of the Bowdoin Bike School, who knew Fritz's neighborhood far better than I. My expertise in presiding at funerals didn't matter much when what we needed was attentiveness to the needs of the neighborhood, not some outsider white pastor running roughshod.

After fumbling through the ceremony, I sat on a nearby stoop with Fritz's family for a while, holding a cousin's hand. With few words between us, we watched as the teenagers came forward to touch Fritz's ghost bike. That was ritual at its best, offering an embodied way to express our deepest longings. And that's what we needed: not the magic fingers of a minister blessing the bike, but the community putting our hands on the bike. Sitting on the stoop, I could see they were creating the ritual I had failed to provide.

Dr. Anita Kurmann, thirty-eight, was killed at an intersection every cyclist in the city knew was dangerous. At the corner of Massachusetts Avenue and Beacon Street, the bike lane disappears exactly where cars often make a right turn. Tragically and predictably, Anita was killed when a truck "right-hooked" her. She was obeying the law and riding in the bike lane. But the driver of a massive flatbed tractor-trailer truck turned right, crossing the bike lane, and hit her. As of this writing, the driver has yet to be identified or charged in Anita's death.

The day of her service, I arrived early to set up and survey the space. From my vantage point at the lamppost, I could see a sort of bicycle honor guard pulling the ghost bike in the trailer behind them. This time the police were there too. I recognized some of the bike cops, and a few of them remembered me from a Blessing of the Bicycles earlier in the summer. Anita was a radiant, talented young doctor about to publish major thyroid research, killed in an intersection we cyclists all biked through in fear. So this service drew a larger crowd, including not only the usual cyclists and the other doctors with whom Anita had worked, but non-cyclists and the press.

I had learned my lesson with Fritz's ghost bike dedication: people need an accessible ritual to grieve well. After the crash but before the ceremony, Anita's mother had come from her home in Switzerland and tied a ribbon in Anita's favorite color—pink— around the lamppost nearest the crash site. The night before the service, the ghost bike guild came up with the idea of passing out pink ribbons to mourners. This time, as I gathered us to dedicate the bike, everyone reached forward, laying a hand on the bike or the shoulder of the person in front of them. As people departed, they came forward to touch the bike and take a ribbon. We ran out of ribbons, visible signs of Anita's life and our own fragility.

Each ghost bike is a visible sign of a life in motion brought to a halt. I think we turn out to dedicate these strangers' ghost bikes so that we also can be seen and signal to other cyclists that we see them, too. Maybe it's an act of witness to make visible the poor road design that puts cyclists in peril. Maybe we turn out as an act of defiance, lighting candles against the wind. City cyclists either choose or are forced to a daily habit of biking that puts us at odds with the majority culture. Though our ranks have tripled in the past decade, only 2.4 percent of Bostonians regularly commute by bike. And among the city's cyclists, women account for only 33 percent of ridership. (Neither of these studies included racial or ethnic breakdowns of the cycling community.) Gathering isn't just a luxury; it's a necessity. We have to gather to be seen. We gather to make ourselves visible because our lives depend on it.

Cyclists have a term for what we do when we need to get seen. When there's no bike lane or the shoulder appears unsafe, a cyclist can "take the lane" and move to the center of it. In fact, cyclists always have "the right to use all public ways in the commonwealth except limited access or express state highways where signs specifically prohibiting bicycles have been posted." (The exact citation is Massachusetts General Laws, Chapter 89, Section 11B, which is especially fun to cite when a motorist is complaining about you taking the lane.)

To believe I am worthy to be seen and to faithfully take steps to be seen is an urban spiritual discipline. On my bike and off it, I'm learning to "take the lane" when others would render me invisible. On our bikes and off them, at all times bound by the community we share, we cyclists learn to get visible.

Chapter 6

Fork | Rest

I advise you not to pray aloud much during your fixed times of prayer. Long speeches often become an occasion for straying.... Busy yourself with keeping your mind in the presence of the Lord. If it strays and withdraws sometimes, do not worry about it. Worrying only serves to distract the mind rather than to call it back to God. The will must recall it gently.

"To the Reverend Mother N . . ."
from Brother Lawrence, undated

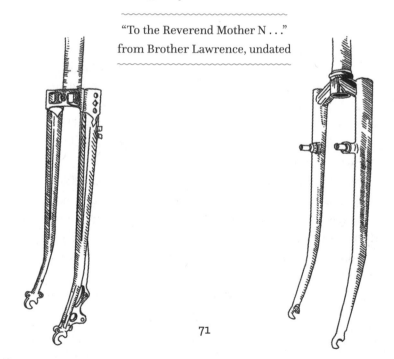

The only way I knew I was really in trouble was the fork. When properly aligned, the front fork holding my front wheel slants away from the bike's frame. But now my fork was slanting backward towards the frame. Looking more closely, I saw that the wheel was bent too. The bent fork was the first indicator that maybe I was really hurt.

When I got hit, I had been riding regularly for about eight months. After the bike sherpas taught me the basics, I took to the bike quickly. I was riding every day and loving it. And I got strong riding that bike. Between my daily bike commute and my yoga practice, I was probably in the best shape I'd been in since college.

I was hit on December 1, 2010—a Wednesday, bright and clear, before the weather had turned really cold. I wasn't heading into my office, but traveling through the city for a meeting—conveniently, with a bunch of evangelicals. After I was hit, I texted a colleague I'd be late. They sprang into prayer until I arrived by bus.

My old apartment had a driveway that slanted from the building down towards Morton Street, a one-way road. I lived on a side street, just parallel to a major road, so some drivers used our street to cut through traffic and speed along.

That day I rolled my bike slowly down the driveway and merged onto the road—and that's when the driver hit the front wheel of Hideki. In retrospect, I was lucky. The crash could have been a lot worse if it had been a direct hit or if I had been moving faster.

As I tumbled off the car's bright white hood and onto the road, I thought, *Head up—keep your head up.* Blessedly, my head never hit the pavement. In fact, I bounced right up, and I think I shouted, "Why the hell did you hit me?" Not my most gracious greeting, but then again, I had just been struck by two tons of steel.

The woman started yelling at me immediately, something like, "You people are always getting in the way." Any sentence that starts with "you people" isn't going to end well. You people with red hair? You people in yellow jackets? I think she meant cyclists, but I wasn't clear-headed enough to ask at the time. And getting in the way of what? I think she meant in the way of cars, or maybe her car, but that presumes a lot about who has priority on our shared roads. I find that drivers often protest that "You came out of nowhere" when they, in fact, should have seen something that was right in front of them. I had looked right before I entered the road, but the driver was speeding around the corner, so that between the time I looked and the time I entered the road, she was already there.

It was cold enough that day that I had put on a bright yellow Gore-Tex shell, not the most flattering color but good for repelling both cars and water. When I fell off the hood of the car onto the road, I ripped open the jacket, rendering it useless against rain. That was just one more thing that made me angry, but what made me angrier still was when the driver later claimed, again and again, that she didn't see me. What was she talking about? Bright yellow jacket, black Spandex leggings—I looked like a freaking parakeet.

The ensuing details about insurance and the aftermath aren't all that interesting. What I didn't realize at the time was how hurt I actually was.

Apart from the tear in my yellow jacket, nothing on my body appeared to rip or break. I would have tried to ride—in fact, I think I did—but I realized that the fork was bent in a direction that made the bike un-rideable. It's possible that the frame was cracked or some other invisible harm was done, but the fork was my first indicator of damage.

It took a few hours for my body's indicators of damage to kick in. I rolled my wounded bike back into my apartment, balancing it on my back wheel since the front fork was bent backwards. I changed out of my bike clothes, grabbed a bus pass, downed some ibuprofen, and took the bus to my meeting. By that night, as my adrenaline wore off, I began to realize that I was in trouble, and the harm done was far worse than I had initially thought.

That night, I looked more carefully at the bike. Its fork was undeniably pushed backwards, the wheel bent. I posted a photo to Facebook, crowdsourcing among my bicycle friends: "Can this bike be saved?"

Forks aren't the most interesting part of the bike, but they're critical. The front fork connects the front wheel to the bike frame. At the bottom, the fork has two prongs on either side of the wheel, connecting to the axle. At the top, the fork connects to the frame via the "headset," which allows the fork to turn and thus enable steering. Like the frame itself, forks can be made of steel, aluminum, titanium, or carbon fiber.

The fork isn't productive in its own right, but it's the connective tissue that allows the bike to roll and steer. Without a fork, the front wheel couldn't pivot and turn. The top part of the fork, known as the steerer tube, is invisible on an assembled bike, concealed inside the head tube of the frame. Like a spinal cord, it runs inside the body of the bike.

The responses to my post rolled in. *Maybe? Possibly? Might not be worth it. Might not be safe.* My steel fork was badly bent from the crash, and there could be invisible cracks in the frame. Of course, steel can be straightened—to a certain extent. The "steel is real" crowd points to this as the reason that their chosen material is superior—any welder anywhere around the world can usually bend your funky fork back into shape. But my fork looked bent too far. So my bike friends advised that a new fork would probably be safer and less ex-

pensive than the labor cost to reshape this one. My concern—
stupidly at this point—was still for my bike, not my body.

The bent fork was an early indicator of a much larger problem: my bike was actually both un-rideable and un-repairable.
But my body took the more serious hit: after the crash, I ended
up with a bulged disk in my spine and a fair amount of fear in
my legs. It would take me a full two years to get back to where
I had been on my bike.

Being hit by the car forced a rest that I wasn't planning to
take. And so began my bicycle sabbath.

It took a while for me to come around to it, but if a sabbath rest is good enough for God, I thought, I expect it's good
enough for me. The idea of sabbath comes from Scripture. In
Genesis, God created the universe in six days, and rested on
the seventh. In Exodus, sabbath came with the liberation of
the enslaved Israelites. When enslaved, the Israelites weren't
in control of their own labor; once free, they could determine
their own rhythm of work and rest. A regular practice of intentional rest resists the pressure of constant labor and constant motion.

Boston has a curious history of bicycles and Sabbath. The
first wave of cyclists were wealthy white men, then women,
who didn't have to work—or work much—and so could head
out on a group ride that lasted a full day and included a stop
or two at a tavern along their scenic route. For a time, the national League of American Wheelmen had rules against Sunday rides and races. These Sabbath prohibitions worked when
cycling was a leisure activity of an elite class who determined
their own schedules of work and rest.

But the second-wave Boston cycling clubs rode headlong
into Massachusetts's Sabbath-protection laws. As mass pro-

duction began and the price of a bicycle dropped, cycling democratized. Soon working-class people of every racial and ethnic community could afford bicycles. They couldn't go on full-day jaunts during the week, but they could go on the one day of the week no one was working: Sunday. At the annual meeting of the New England Sabbath Protective League in 1899, a speaker railed, "Workmen who have bicycles and use them on Sunday, so that they come to their Monday's work thoroughly tired out, cheat their employers out of an honest day's labor."

Curiously, while cyclists used to be at the forefront of breaking the Sunday Sabbath laws in greater Boston, now some bike shops are upholding Sabbath rest for their workers in a new way. I first noticed this at Hub Bicycle in Cambridge, where the owner, Emily Thibodeau, closes on Sundays. A number of smaller, less corporate bike shops are following this practice so that both owners and employees can go out for a ride, road or mountain. These are the shops that live what they sell. Rather than keep employees working on a beautiful Sunday when sales are maximized but joy is minimized, they make sure that their workers can be out riding. I've heard more than a few mountain bikers call their Sunday-morning ride "church." Back during the first cycling boom of the early twentieth century, Harvard President Charles Eliot countered the sentiments of the New England Sabbath Protective League by saying, "God delights in every innocent pleasure. I ride a bicycle or a horse for pleasure on Sunday, without feeling that I have desecrated the Sabbath Day."

In the beginning, my bicycle sabbatical was like living under those Puritanical laws on a never-ending Sunday: no fun and no movement. There was nothing spiritually transcendent about my rest; in fact, I was kind of an insufferable jerk through most of it. I had just found this glorious way of moving through the world even faster than I had before, and suddenly I was stopped cold. My dead car had been donated to the local public radio station, and my bike was unsalvageable. I returned to the throngs who packed the #39 bus and the Orange Line on Boston's subway. Gone was the pleasure of moving at my own speed, on my own route, going where I wanted when I wanted. Now I was dependent on other people to take me where I wanted to go, on their schedule, when they wanted.

I didn't think of myself as crazy-busy, but I certainly was moving through my life at a fairly fast clip when I got hit. In a flash, I was off my bike and out of yoga at a stressful time in my life. My yoga practice and my bike commute had become my daily go-to stress relievers, and now they were gone. And not only was I dependent upon other people to shuttle me around, but I was in serious pain—another freaking reminder of my humanity. I had grossly underappreciated the benefit of a healthy spine until mine was compromised. With my active life screeched to a stop, my bicycle sabbath was a restless stillness.

So it will come as no surprise that I—foolishly—tried to ride before my body was sufficiently rested. Like trying to travel before the roads are plowed of snow, it can be done, but it's much harder than necessary. I was anxious to get back on the bike for fear of having the scare set in if I stayed off too long after the crash. I had been in physical therapy to build back some of the strength I had lost and had gotten a steroid injection into my spine, so I was feeling a bit better. But mostly, I was restless.

I borrowed a bicycle from a friend, repacked my dusty pannier with my work clothes, and saddled up. The first few miles I rode like a toddler, wobbly and slow. I stopped at every light; I let every car pass until it was absolutely clear to go. A commute that used to take me a swift thirty minutes flat bloated into a clumsy forty-seven minutes. But I did it. I made it to my office, locked the bike up against the lamppost, bent over to remove my pannier—and froze. I couldn't stand up at more than a ninety-degree angle. Somehow I managed to get into my office, mumble something to the secretary, and quickly close my door so I could lie down on the floor, Spandex and all, to try and get the spasm to stop. With obscene amounts of Advil and the heating pack I was now leaving in my office, I managed to make it through the day at an angle. Sheepishly, I texted Abbi, who I had begun to date, and asked for a car ride home.

Since my office wouldn't allow me to bring the bike inside, Abbi unlocked it and threw it into her trunk, then scooped me up and put me into the back of her hatchback so that I could lie down during the ride home. In pain and embarrassed that I couldn't even ride seven miles without calling for help, I lay there stewing that the trip took fifty-five minutes in car traffic but would have been just thirty by bike.

This happened more than once. I'd get restless, try to ride, strain my back again, and then be forced back into rest and more medical interventions. Gentleness with one's body is a new discipline for me, one I've learned slowly and with a fair amount of protest.

I had not made peace with my limitations. Brother Lawrence, on the other hand, experienced his ailments as a way of knowing that he was a finite and limited human. His infirmities brought him closer to Jesus's experience of human suffering. As he was dying, Brother Lawrence is said to have repeated again and again, "My God, I adore you in my infirmities. O my Lord, I can finally suffer something for you. Wonderful! Thank you! Let me suffer and die with you." This was not my experience. I shouted the name of God far more often in anger and pain than in praise for my injuries. "This is bullshit, Lord," was far more frequently my response. If this was what Brother Lawrence meant when he said "we must behave very simply with God, and speak frankly to Him, asking Him for help in things as they happen," then I excelled in speaking frankly to God. "Fix me—now" became my daily prayer, as I lay flat again on the floor.

Though we have a tendency to treat our bikes like fellow humans or pets, the bicycle is a machine that doesn't need rest. Unlike a horse that needs food and sleep, or a car that needs gas, a bike needs neither sleep nor fuel. But we do. The earliest ads touted the bicycle as a "freedom machine" that allowed riders to go wherever they wanted. And I realized I had been treating my body too much like a bike. Now my injuries were trying to teach me that my body needed starts and stops, rest and recovery, that it had limits. Violating these limits kept depositing me, prone, into the back seat of a car, stewing.

Even though Boston is a smaller city, it moves quickly and constantly. But we humans aren't designed for constant motion. Cultivating quiet and stillness might be the spiritual practice with the largest gap between city living and rural life. Because I'm surrounded by constant motion, developing a "thick" spiritual life in the city requires me to find a calm, still center. But that's not easy. Even if I've managed to get myself sitting still in my own apartment, the city pulses just outside my window, the constant beeping of buses backing up punctuated by the low rumble of mopeds. Even if I've found a quiet corner in a city park, other people move just beyond the edge of my vision. The city simply isn't designed for stillness.

Maybe we greet snowstorms that shut down the city temporarily with such glee because we really do want to rest and need external forces to prompt it. But how do we find rest in the city in August? How do we find calm while the chaos of the city churns? Sometimes we get stillness without peace, an uneasy stillness.

Boston cyclists hook on to another event to finally find quiet roads. The night before the Boston Marathon, when 26.2 miles of road are blocked off from traffic, thousands of cyclists make their way out to the starting line in Hopkinton. The "Midnight Marathon" ride starts at twelve A.M. and follows the runners' route into the city. In order to find some peace from the onslaught of traffic, cyclists ride after almost all the cars have left the road. But this happens just once a year, an exception to our everyday lives. So we still search for a sustainable peace and stillness in the city.

Following the 2013 Boston Marathon bombing, my city experienced an enforced stillness. I adore the Boston Marathon, a public, world-class competition, free for spectators, where the elite and the amateur alike run in towards the city, not away from it. Breaking the anonymity of the city, runners write their names on their arms or chests, and the crowd cheers them on by name. But in 2013, all of this was shattered.

The bombing happened on a Monday. On Thursday, I rode my bike downtown to participate in a community prayer service. By late Thursday night, our collective mourning and confusion were sliced through by slivers of breaking news—a car chase, a shooting, possibly a lead to suspects. A *Boston Globe* reporter used a Hubway bike-share bike to follow the story as the chase moved from Boston to Cambridge to Watertown at three in the morning.

On Friday morning the city woke to find we were on "lockdown." Official word was that all Boston residents were to "shelter-in-place," as police went on a "manhunt" to find the bombers. The public transit system was shut down. It was a bright, clear April day, warm enough that we could have sat outside. Instead, in my apartment, my neighbors and I huddled around our computers, constantly hitting "refresh" to see if we could learn anything more.

What I remember most from this time was the quiet. A weekday in the city had never been so silent. The buses didn't beep. The mopeds didn't roar. Most distinctive of all was the complete lack of sound from the train tracks. Even from my apartment, I can distinguish the sound of a local train from a higher speed commuter train. But all that was gone. The only sounds were the occasional police and news helicopters buzzing overhead. I had never heard my city so quiet for so long. The constant movement nearly stopped. But there was no peace in this stillness.

When the "shelter-in-place" order was lifted, we rode our bikes to a local pizza place; all that enforced isolation prompted us to seek out other people in a public space. I had a slice of pizza dangling in my hand when the TV announced that a suspect was being captured. The city was slowly coming back into motion, but the uneasiness remained. It took me two years not to flinch at the sound of a helicopter overhead.

The bombing accentuated the truth that a peaceful stillness is hard to find. Sometimes the city feels like a crowded house where every room has two or three siblings already in it. I once found a quiet corner of the Boston Public Library only to have the stillness interrupted by another patron clipping his fingernails. So where do we go? If no place is quiet, where do we find stillness? If we can't find an outward peace in the loud and crowded city, we turn inward. We seek an internal peace, a peace that transcends circumstance.

In the anxious stillness of my bicycle sabbatical, I was more caged than calm. A true sabbath rest aligns an economy of movement with a stillness of mind. Technically, I was moving more slowly, but my mind kept racing. A true sabbath rest invites thanks for the work behind and restoration for the work ahead, a pivot point around which the rest of the week rotates. Like the bicycle fork, the practice of regular sabbath, crucial but under-appreciated, allows the rest of our lives to move smoothly forward.

True rest from work well done is pleasant, gratifying. We feel what we call "a good tired." It's like a cool drink on the back porch after a long ride when there's nothing left in your legs. Observant Jews mark the beginning of Shabbat by singing and welcoming in the "Sabbath Queen." I welcomed my enforced rest with resentment and foot-stomping. Embracing sabbath rest was a spiritual practice that came hard and slow to me. I was no Brother Lawrence.

Brother Lawrence's internal stillness was practiced and familiar, even as the world around him clattered and clanged, not in a city but in a monastery kitchen. Brother Lawrence's peaceful devotion to God was "so familiar that he used to say that it seemed impossible to turn aside from it and be concerned with anything else." His peacefulness came not from the absence of external chaos, or an internal void, but from a spirit filled with God. His intimacy with God was such that he said, "I possess God as tranquility in the noise and clatter of my kitchen, where sometimes several people ask me different things at the same time."

Brother Lawrence's answer was not to flee to the quiet

of a church, but to find a peace and a stillness in the present, inside himself. Whatever chaos besets us, Brother Lawrence says, we can find peace within: "We do not have to be constantly in church to be with God. We can make our heart a prayer room into which we can retire from time to time to converse with God gently, humbly, and lovingly."

Brother Lawrence believed that our daily lives are our mindful acts of devotion. And that there are also times when we need to silence ourselves. It's hard to hear what anyone else is saying if we're talking all the time. Brother Lawrence directs us to hold ourselves silently before God, as if we were unable to speak. Into that silence, wherever we find it, we go to listen. That is our spiritual discipline.

At first I entered the silence to complain, not to listen. It was unfair that my bike was ruined and that I wouldn't be compensated. It was unfair that my body was wounded, and that some careless driver was still going on her merry way, blindly speeding around corners. My unrequested sabbatical brought a restless stillness before it brought peace. But sometime during those two years, when I was lying once again on the floor to ease my back pain, I knew I was at a crossroads: Either I could fight this enforced stillness, or I could surrender to this season and heal. So I surrendered, and in the process I embraced this quieting spiritual practice in my noisy city. In the quiet, I noticed more than my back was in pain.

The spiritual life is a process of becoming aware of the places where we are more hurt than we realize, and doing what needs to be done to heal. For me, that process required resting, physically and spiritually, and only later getting back on the bike.

Chapter 7

Handlebars | Adaptation

He had fulfilled his kitchen duties with the greatest love possible for a period of about thirty years, until Providence ordained otherwise. A large ulcer appeared on his leg, obliging his superiors to assign him to an easier office. This change gave him more leisure to adore God in spirit and in truth and more time to occupy himself more totally with His pure presence by the practice of faith and love.

from Brother Lawrence's Eulogy by the Abbé of Beaufort

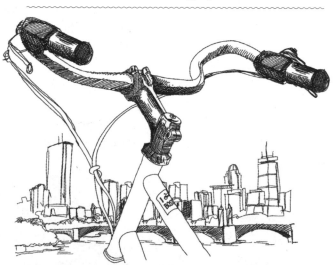

Finally, the wait was over, but I had no bike. I had slogged through nearly two years of recovery and re-injury, multiple steroid shots in my spine, hours of physical therapy, acupuncture, embarrassing purchases of old-people supplies from pharmacies still owned by a single family, and a nightly ritual of lying on the apartment floor to stretch out my back. Now I could stand upright again. I was ready, tentatively, to return to the road. But Hideki, my swift single-speed Club Fuji bike, was not.

In Abbi's basement, we stripped Hideki for parts. We performed a bicycle autopsy, deciding what could be transplanted to another bike and what was too far gone. The front fork was bent and unredeemable. The steel frame, though it had minimal visible damage, might have internal cracks that would make it unsafe to re-use. To make a commemorative bottle opener, Abbi took a hacksaw to the red frame to cut off the chainstay, the tapered steel tube between the bottom bracket and the dropouts. I went to work taking apart the rest of the bike.

The impact of the car had folded the front wheel in half, a collision result evocatively known as being "taco-ed." The pedals, crank, and handlebars could all be salvaged for use on another bike. Even before the crash, I knew the hub was getting close to being shot, so that went into the scrap pile. I saved the saddle for myself, even though it wasn't worth much. I had spent hours, even weeks in that saddle, and a good-fitting saddle is hard to find. Lights and grips and fenders—every little thing that we could take, we did.

When we had finished picking at this red bird, we took a step back from the stand. It looked naked now, stripped of all its parts. As we stood before the remains of this roadkill, I started to cry. Hideki had carried me through this city and helped me become a Bostonian. Now, all that was left was what the neighborhood guys would take to sell for scrap. I knew a bike of such seminal importance needed a better burial than this. So we cracked open two beers with the commemorative steel chainstay and raised them up. "To Hideki," Abbi said. "To Hideki," I blubbered.

And so, after the post-mortem on Hideki, the hunt for the new bicycle began. During that economic discipleship Bible study, I had opened up a "bicycle sinking fund." Out of every paycheck each month, ten dollars had dropped into this savings account. Now I actually had some money to work with to find a new bike. My bike-builder friends began to scheme. Complete bicycles can be purchased from bike shops and department stores and the Internet and garage sales. But far more interesting is the process of building a bicycle.

Whereas Hideki was a hand-me-down, this bike would begin as mine. Abbi and my friend Erich, who worked at a local bike shop, would build it, in exchange for a number of home-cooked meals and hand-sewn bicycle caps. I thought this was an excellent deal. Somewhere in our trade negotiations, I signed off on letting Abbi and Erich pick the colors. This would result in my ultimately riding a ridiculous bicycle with bubble-gum pink tires, which amused Abbi and Erich to no end.

The first goal was to re-use what we already had, an ethic that, when pushed to its natural end, becomes known as building a "Frankenbike." We could use the Mavic wheels I had inherited when Mark died. A few small items could be transplanted from Hideki: the stem, the saddle, the seat post, and the quick-release skewer which connects the wheel to the front fork through the axle. We walked down the street to Bikes Not Bombs, the community bike shop, to scavenge through their second-hand bin and came home with a new (to me) crank.

For the rest, my bike friends recommended the parts, and we used my bicycle fund to pay for them. We had some money to play with, but not a lot. With bicycle parts, the aphorism goes: "Light, strong, cheap—pick any two." For my new commuter bike, designed to endure daily use and being locked up outside, we mostly chose strong and cheap. We ordered a steel Pake commuter frame, like the one Erich rode daily. Slowly, the pieces were coming together. But we were still missing a crucial item: the right handlebars.

On the earliest bicycles, the handlebars were made from a solid bar of steel, hence "handlebar." Still called the same, modern handlebars are made from tubes of a strong material in one of two broad categories, depending on where they place you: drop or upright. Handlebars guide the bicycle's steering system, comprised of handlebars, handlebar stem, headset, and front fork. The headset allows the front fork (and therefore the front wheel) to turn independently from the frame, allowing for the all-important ability to steer.

When I bought Hideki, he had the original drop handlebars. Curved like rams' horns, the drop bars are standard on most road bikes, and for good reason—you can move your hands to multiple positions while steering and adapt to the terrain. Cyclist Robert Penn praises this variety over a long haul: "You can sit up with your hands on the flat 'tops' and admire the view; you can rest your hands on the 'ramps' and slipstream the rider in front; hook your hands around the ends and wrench up the steepest inclines out of the saddle; or shove your fists into the Ds and spring for the line or hare down a mountainside."

When I was first learning to ride in the city, we swapped out Hideki's original drop bars for flat handlebars. Flat bars originated with mountain bikes, since the primary objective while riding over tree trunks and rocks is maneuverability, not aerodynamics. Increasingly, flat bars are used for city riding on commuter and hybrid bikes. The sleek, fixed-gear bikes favored by bike messengers will often have very narrow flat bars, which allow them to slip in between lanes of traffic without getting their handlebars caught on a car's side mirror. Highrise handlebars of some variation are most often seen on BMX, low-rider, and beach-cruiser bicycles. Designed for bicycles carrying lots of gear over long distances, touring or "butterfly" handlebars make an almost complete loop, the tube wrapping back around in front of the stem. Triathlon competitors and insufferable cyclists who are trying to turn their daily commute into a time trial will affix "aero" bars to allow their arms to come together over the front wheel for maximum speed (and minimal ability to brake quickly). The variations are nearly endless: bullhorn bars, mustache bars, albatross bars, and the hybrid "albastache" bars, all sounding like hipster cocktail options. There's a handlebar for every type of cyclist.

On the long road back to daily commuting, none of the handlebars described were quite right for me. So Abbi and Erich suggested something a little less aggressive, a little more upright: North Road handlebars.

I had no idea what they meant. Bicycles have a vocabulary all their own, and I was still learning. Erich pulled up a picture of the North Road bars on his phone, the handlebars typical of an English three-speed bicycle.

"I'll look like the Wicked Witch of the West!" I protested.

"Yes, you will," Abbi replied. "But your back will thank you."

Not surprisingly, Abbi and Erich were right. Although I tended to look like Mary Poppins toddling along on my new bike, the upright handlebars that swept back towards my body did make my ride more comfortable after my back injury.

Cyclists can spend hours debating proper bicycle geometry and "fit." But recall the three basic points of contact between a rider and her bike: feet, hands, and butt. Bikes can be built to move those three endpoints of a triangle closer or farther apart and put them at different angles. In general, with handlebars, you want your hands in line with your shoulders, leaving your chest open to breathe easily.

The North Road bars were a wise adaptation, probably one I wouldn't have considered on my own. But after my crash, I faced a new reality: I wasn't as strong through my core, and my back wasn't as comfortable when stretched out. The upright bars were kinder and gentler on my body. If I wanted to get back to commuting every day, I'd take and make what adaptations I needed to get there.

One of the hallmarks of cities is adaptation, specifically adaptation of space and buildings. Despite all the concrete and steel, cities are flexible spaces over time; a shortage of space means that places have multiple lives and multiple uses. Boston's Franklin Park, designed by Frederick Law Olmstead, once had space for lawn tennis and croquet—space now turned into parking lots and football fields. Harvard Yard once had an area dedicated to cattle-grazing that now serves as an outdoor lounge for students. In my neighborhood, an old brewery is now a café, an old warehouse is now a business incubator, an old church is now a school, and an old school is now a condo complex. Cities are constantly adapting old spaces for new uses, sometimes to great effect and sometimes with massive wounding to the community. Bostonians in particular have a habit of navigating based on what used to be, so they'll give directions like "Go down Winter Street past where Locke Ober used to be and then take a left in front of where

Filene's Basement used to be." This habit isn't particularly helpful to new residents, but it does tell you something about how deeply ingrained those old spaces are, even after they've been adapted into something new. As cities constantly adapt, the spiritual practice required of city residents is adaptation.

Constraints make for creativity. When space is constrained, cities build up, over, and around. When space is expendable, cities sprawl. I recognize this shows my East Coast urban bias, but I'll take a weird, tucked-away ally in Boston or Philly any day over the sidewalk-less sprawl of Atlanta or Los Angeles. Constraints require cities to get creative within parameters, like poets within the structure of a sonnet. At a city level, adaptability means constantly asking how to re-use or re-imagine buildings and places. At a personal level, city living requires that we learn to adapt to the changing landscape and changing population. Or, put negatively, living so close to so many other people means learning to live flexibly with those you cannot control. In a city, you can't put up "no trespassing" signs on the acres around your home to buffer yourself from others. Urban living asks us to adapt to the constant flux of people and the ceaseless change of cities. Curiously, cities invite us to be both stable and flexible, often at the same time.

Like a city, a monastery offers the spiritual practice of living in close proximity with many others. To live in such a space requires a personal flexibility to keep that vow of stability. After thirty years in the monastery kitchen, peeling potatoes while practicing the presence of God, Brother Lawrence fell ill. With a wounded leg, he couldn't stand as easily and so was assigned a less labor-intensive job. The Abbé of Beaufort observed that the injury afforded Brother Lawrence "more leisure to adore God in spirit and in truth and more time to occupy himself more totally with His pure presence by the practice of faith and love." He adapted to his injury and his new job in ways that invited more grace.

I was surprised to find more grace in my adaptation to a different set of handlebars. Mostly I was worried that I'd look like a caricature of a demure Victorian woman sitting daintily upright on a bicycle, not the street-savvy, urban-warrior cyclist I imagined myself to be. And I did look different—but I could also see differently. The new upright bars raised my head and, more precisely, my eyes. Now I could see a bit more of the city around me.

So, yes, the North Road handlebars looked a bit ridiculous, but they also provided an enjoyable ride. I wouldn't win any races behind them, but something about the posture and the cultural association made it fun to toddle along. I was sitting upright, arms stretched out before me. This is how I returned to the road, a slightly slower and chastened cyclist. With these new handlebars, I found myself a bit more patient with those around me and a bit more willing to steer wide.

To co-exist in the city, we learn to steer around one another. We have choices about how we do it. There's an emerging code of conduct for cyclists about how we pass one another. Calling out "on your left" is the traditional signal that you're going to pass and overtake a slower cyclist, pedestrian, or wild turkey (many of which frequent the genteel neighborhoods of Brookline). Others use their bike bells to give people a heads-up, a signal that generally works for all without presuming a shared language. Wobbly toddlers and puppy dogs tend not to obey any of the rules of the road, and so it's wise to steer wide around their unpredictable path. In theory, the rules for multi-use bike and pedestrian paths are like those for mall escalators—pass on the left; keep slower traffic on the right. But anyone who's navigated an airport people-mover knows that these rules aren't universally followed. So on the road, cyclists learn to ride defensively, aiming to be dependable ourselves and leaving enough margin for undependable others.

Sometimes other travelers are clumsy or unaware of how their movements affect others—and some people are just jerks. I have the unhelpful habit of taking this as a personal insult. Every cyclist has a story or seven to tell about the indignity of being passed by a speed demon, only to get stuck behind that same demon when he or she can't maintain their speed. Every cyclist who has one of these stories also has a companion story about how damn good it felt to just sit behind said demon, cruising along and making them work all the harder.

Boston doesn't have many sections of dependable gridded streets like New York or Chicago. But on a small stretch of Commonwealth Avenue in the Back Bay, there are stoplights at regular intervals. If you time it just right, you can skate the lights and ride without stopping from Arlington Street to Berkley Street to Clarendon Street, and through the alphabet until the whole game ends at Massachusetts Avenue. I was happily cruising along in this area one spring evening after work—until I realized that a certain cyclist was running the red lights, but actually riding slowly enough that I was catching and overtaking him in between each intersection. He would run the red light, and I would catch him, from Arlington to Berkley, from Berkley to Clarendon, from Clarendon to Dartmouth, over and over again. Once I figured out what was happening, I had something to prove (smugness is a contagious disease among cyclists): my legs were faster than his disregard for traffic lights. So in between every light that he had just blown through, I passed him. Now, I could have just let it go, and not turned a mile-long stretch of road into an epic battle between good and evil. I probably deserved it when I got to Massachusetts Avenue first, and he passed me on the inside (illegally) to make a right turn. Looking back over his left shoulder, he shouted "Jackass!" I was right: my legs were faster than his rule-breaking. But he was also right: I was being a jackass.

Practical cycling gives us multiple opportunities every day to resist the temptation to be a jackass. This isn't easy, but it's an urban spiritual discipline that's important to maintain.

When cyclists queue up at stoplights, most of the female cyclists I know are routinely passed, an annoying habit known as "shoaling." Bike Snob explains: "Instead of stopping behind you, as is the basis of all other line formation in modern Western society, the rider passes you and stops in front of you." Then another and another cyclist does the same. Shoaling happens all the time, but it's particularly galling when some dude cuts off a whole group of cyclists waiting patiently in line. I believe this is called "entitlement," no longer just a metaphor but the very privilege that presumes you get to go to the front of the line. Again, I have a bad habit of taking this personally, as if this cyclist assumes he's faster than me just because I'm riding in a skirt. Either the cyclist is completely oblivious to the line of fellow humans queued up as if waiting at Dunkin' Donuts, or he thinks he deserves to cut the line, lest he lose three seconds in the commuter time trial. Certain cyclists think they're owed a pole position.

This and the other indignities I've detailed are the city trying to bait me into behaving badly. Resistance is hard. Flexibility is required. A mature urban spirituality would advise that I remain non-reactive and use my fancy new handlebars just to steer wide. But sometimes cyclists are *forced* to steer around, even when we have the right of way. Then we're confronted with the advanced commuter decision: Do I want to be right, or do I want to be alive?

Sometimes, even when we have the right of way, it's absurd *not* to steer around. In 2011 the New York Police Department began a crackdown, and suddenly everyday cyclists were getting tickets for things like "not having bells on their bikes and not wearing helmets (even though there's no law requiring adults to wear helmets)." In the dragnet, filmmaker Casey Neistat was snagged and ticketed by an NYPD officer for not riding in the bike lane. Every urban cyclist on earth, including every police officer on the bicycle beat, knows how impossible it is to only ride in the bike lane, a space that apparently communicates to some drivers a reserved spot for their double parking.

Neistat's response? He had a friend film his attempt to *only* ride in the bike lane. The video tracks Neistat's "painful-looking pratfalls as he crashed into obstructions, including a moving truck and a police cruiser, like a modern-day Buster Keaton," according to *The New York Times*. (It's no surprise that this video now has almost eighteen million YouTube views.) In typically blunt New York fashion, the city's share-the-road education campaign was self-evidently titled "Don't Be a Jerk." I suspect if Boston's Transit Department initiated a similar campaign, it would draw on our cultural norms of passive-aggressive shaming and avoidance: "We see you being a jerk, and we're gonna tell your mom."

One night coming home late from a work event along Columbus Avenue, I noticed the car in front of me driving erratically. First the driver would hug the shoulder, as if trolling for a parking spot along the line of parked cars, then drift towards the center lines, not crossing over, but brushing the yellow before driving back. I could have sped up and tried to pass, but it seemed safer to hold back. Finally the driver turned right onto Massachusetts Avenue as I went straight ahead. I stewed the rest of my ride home. Did they drop something on the floor? Were they texting? Something was distracting the driver. Only about a block from my home did it click: the driver was probably drunk. I hadn't paid enough attention to the license plate to alert the police. Were other cyclists and motorists now in danger since I didn't report this? My adaptive strategy for dealing with an erratic driver like this is usually to hang back and give them a wide berth. It's better to be alive than to be fast.

Adaptation isn't just a personal spiritual discipline, but a communal one. The Southwest Corridor, the bike path I travel almost every day, is a parable of adaptation and stability, a jeremiad of both loss and resistance. Some days I travel roads along ancient cow paths and over landfills. Along the Southwest Corridor, I travel over the ruins of bulldozed homes and a failed highway.

Flush with funds from the 1956 Defense Interstate Highway Act, Boston went on a highway building spree, including building the elevated Central Artery highway, which would be torn down fifty years later in the boondoggle known as "The Big Dig." Two major, elevated highways were proposed: the Inner Belt ring road and the Southwest Expressway. Initially, everyone seemed onboard: the "City Fathers," the Chamber of Commerce, and all the newspapers. The proposed Southwest Expressway would create a new, elevated eight-lane highway over eight miles, bifurcating the neighborhoods of Hyde Park, Jamaica Plain, Roxbury, and the South End before connecting to another highway. To build the expressway, the city would need to forcibly remove over two thousand households—a pretty shitty thing to do to one's neighbors. Proof that not all urban adaptations should be met with flexibility.

The neighborhoods got educated, got angry, and got organized, culminating in a massive "People before Highways" rally on Boston Common on January 25, 1969. The opposition coalition reflected the diversity of the city. While successful in stopping the highway, the opposition couldn't stop the destruction. As people had organized and strategized, the Department of Public Works had seized homes; already twelve hundred had been taken, many in Lower Roxbury, for a highway that would never be built. At the time, *The Boston Globe* transportation reporter blithely commented, "You can't build an enormous eight-lane super-road through four crowded communities without hurting someone," and suggested modern mitigations like landscaping to muffle the proposed highway's sounds. Although the super-road was never built, many people were hurt, and not just by noise pollution. The city didn't try to steer wide around the residents of these neighborhoods, instead steamrolling those blocking the route it felt entitled to take. The city was a drunk driver, taking out parked cars in its path.

The people stopped the highway, but the homes were already gone. With the "Boston Provision" of the Federal Aid Highway Act of 1973, states could use federal highway money for public transit. The seized land and the new funds led to the creation of the below-ground Orange Line Subway and the Southwest Corridor bike path.

For the first year that I traveled this path on Hideki, all of this history was hidden to me. When I returned to the path on my new bike with my upright handlebars and my eyes cast higher, I finally noticed a small monument at the Roxbury Crossing MBTA station, detailing the history buried beneath the path I was riding.

After the "People before Highways" rally, Massachusetts Governor Frank Sargent "promised he wouldn't 'make decisions that place people below concrete.'" Nearly fifty years later, there are people, entire lives and histories and homes, below the concrete under my wheels. On the city's bike map today, the Southwest Corridor boasts a bright pink line indicating its high value as a protected bike path physically separated from car traffic. That pink line, a five-mile straight shot into the center of the city, is part of what allowed me to begin biking. But I ride on scar tissue. There was adaptation, but not without cost.

Adaptation is a constant in the spiritual life. Sometimes a spiritual discipline that previously worked well may not work any longer. Adaptation trusts that we can find another route.

Chapter 8

Gears | Pacing

Although his duties were great and difficult, when he alone did the duties that two brothers usually did, he was never seen to act with haste. Rather, with exactness and moderation, he gave each thing the time it required, always maintaining his modest and tranquil manner. He worked neither slowly nor hastily, remaining in constant evenness of mind and in unchanging peace.

from Brother Lawrence's Eulogy by the Abbé of Beaufort

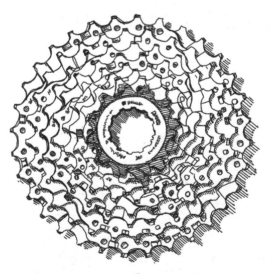

All my life, pacing has been a struggle. In automotive terms, I idle too high. In many settings, this is a socially advantageous addiction. I've yet to have an employer who really protested "You work too fast" and helped me slow down. But personally, this fast pace is a problem. A few years ago, a therapist keenly observed, "You seem to have two settings: high speed and complete stop, and you don't use the second very much."

This is a genuine struggle that has also affected my relationships. Moving fast, I try to cram in too many things. I remember trying to schedule a time to hang out with my friend Braden, suggesting that we could try a new recipe together, or re-wire a broken lamp I had found, or plant some perennials in my garden. Braden gently countered, "We could just hang out without a project, too." My younger sister Kate longs for the day when I'll just sit on the couch with her to watch a movie and not also bring with me some beans to be hulled or some needlepoint I could simultaneously stitch. In more recent years, when friends inquire about my bicycle habit, Abbi teasingly responds, "I didn't create this monster—I just put it on a bike."

Since I can't really do more than one thing at a time on a bicycle, my bike is one of the few things that forces me to maintain a singular focus. In the old days, before smart phones and before my bike, I would commute to work by subway or bus, listening to music on headphones while simultaneously reading the newspaper. Commuting by bike is complicated enough. I know other cyclists make a different decision, but I won't wear headphones while I ride, since I need the audio clues about the traffic around me. The bike does manage to work a little of my extra energy out of me— what a good walk does for a puppy. But because I "idle high," the bike initially gave me a whole new way to keep moving fast through life.

My first bike, Hideki, was a single-speed with just one gear, so its movement was entirely dependent on the strength of my legs. If I wanted to go faster, I had to pedal faster. If I wanted to climb a hill, I had to push harder. I found this direct connection between my power and the bike's speed enormously gratifying. With a single-speed, you just get on and go. Since you're only in one gear, you're always in the right gear.

There's a certain bravado accorded to those riding just one gear. In fact, the founder of the Tour de France was a proponent of single-gear bikes not just because of their simplicity, but because they were a sign of strength and fortitude. Henri Desgranges, an editor whose promotion of the Tour became a (successful) newspaper marketing scheme, wrote, "Variable gears are only for people over forty-five. Isn't it better to triumph by the strength of your muscles rather than by the artifice of a derailleur? We are getting soft."

There are multiple reasons why cyclists either choose or convert to single-speed bicycles, including the aforementioned machismo attributed to them. Cyclists known as "weight weenies" are obsessed with making their bikes as light as possible, so getting rid of additional gears and shifters is one option. Pragmatic cyclists figure that gears and derailleurs which move the chain onto the gears are just more components to rust, bend, break, and fail, especially on bikes often locked outside. Then there are those who appreciate the psychological satisfaction of riding a single-speed bike. Human velo-encyclopedia Sheldon Brown wrote, "Riding a single speed can help bring back the unfettered joy you experienced riding your bike as a child. You don't realize how much mental energy you devote to shifting until you relinquish your derailleurs, and discover that a whole corner of your brain that was formerly wondering when to shift is now free to enjoy your surroundings and sensations."

All that said, a single-speed isn't the most efficient type of bicycle to ride. For maximum speed and distance with minimum effort, you want a bike with gears.

Single-speed bikes come in two varieties: free-wheel and fixed-wheel. A "free" rear wheel is able to turn without the pedals moving, and the rider can simply coast. A "fixed" wheel can't coast. If the bike is rolling, the pedals are turning. Fixed-gear bikes, or "fixies," have a cult-like devotion, and in truth, they're great fun to ride. Some converts claim a "one-ness with the bike that is not equaled by a freewheeling bike." Another devotee swoons, "Riding one [a brakeless fixie] well in city traffic makes you a high priest in the Cult of Equipment."

I haven't ascended to this high priesthood, but I have embraced the fun and simplicity of riding a single-speed bike. In the first six months of riding Hideki, I rode hard and often. By summer, I had ridden the bike so hard and so often that the teeth on the front chain ring and the rear free-wheel had worn down into a sharpened mess. At the same time, I had become stronger. When Abbi and I replaced the chain and the free-wheel, we bumped me up to a bigger chain ring. This meant that the bike needed more of my energy to pedal and get going—and I could go even faster. I took gleeful pride in this upgrade.

On an early ride with Erich and Abbi, I joined them on their commute to the bike store in the burbs—what used to be International Bicycle, but now is Landry's. (Note my Bostonian milestone: describing a new place based on what it used to be!) They were both riding bikes with gears while I pedaled single-speed Hideki. We moved easily together through the flat neighborhood before crossing the Arborway to leave Jamaica Plain and head northwest towards the bike shop.

As we turned the corner, the hill up Pond Street loomed

in front of us. Unused to riding with other people, I did what I had learned to do every morning riding up Beacon Hill on my own: attack. I was driven by my crude philosophy: Riding uphill is very painful, so get it over with as soon as possible. So I charged, staying seated as long as I could before standing up in the pedals, loath to lose the momentum I had gained in getting the wheels to spin as the resistance up the hill increased. It wasn't pretty, but it worked. As Pond Street flattened out and turned into Newton Street, I realized I was alone.

Erich and Abbi pulled up alongside me, looking calm and collected as I was still catching my breath. "What was that?" Erich asked. "Were you trying to win King of the Mountain?" I wasn't trying to show off; I just didn't know what else to do. "King" or "Queen of the Mountain" is the title bestowed on the best climber in big road races. A red-and-white polka-dot jersey, or the "maillot à pois rouge," is bestowed on these mountain royals, though the jersey looks more like something worn by a court jester than a king. I think if you're bad-ass enough to win King of the Mountain, you can withstand looking like a clown in a polka-dot jersey.

I saw Erich's point. I rode like a novice, expending all of my energy to get up the hill instead of pacing myself. If I had been riding a bike with gears, I could have downshifted to an easier gear so that my legs were still moving at the same pace even as the road got harder. I also could have just slowed down and not bombed the hill. And, to be clear, we're talking about a hill here, and a Boston hill at that—not exactly the Alpe d'Huez of the Tour de France mountain stages.

Later on, Abbi commented, "It seems your general philosophy of life is 'If it's difficult, push harder.'" Sometimes, the wiser thing to do is shift. Cyclists have a mantra for this: "Shift, don't grind." The prospect of shifting reminds me that I need not grind my way through every hardship.

And indeed, I was forced to downshift after getting hit.

The long road back to recovery took some of the frenetic energy out of me, but mostly it got rechanneled to new places. Still, I came back to the bike a little more humble, a little more chagrined. And Abbi, Erich, and I built my second bicycle with gears.

My second bike, the pink-and-gray commuter build, has twenty-seven gears—specifically, Shimano's Tiagra HG50 9-Speed Road Cassette. The bike has three rings in the front and nine cogs in the back for a total of twenty-seven possible gears. Twenty-seven is probably more than I actually need. I sometimes still ride as if I were on a single-speed, staying in my middle gears and not messing with shifting. But multiple gears do allow me a bit more precision and efficiency on the road. I can shift into a lower gear to make climbing a hill easier. I can shift into a higher gear to take advantage of my momentum.

Now it's time for a biking confession: shortly after building my geared commuter bike, I acquired another single-speed. I was back in New Jersey visiting my parents, and the town library where I had my first job was having a rummage sale. There, pulled from the depths of someone's basement, was a mid-80s Club Fuji road bike, with an asking price of just fifteen dollars! In Boston, where used bicycles (and old bicycles scavenged from basements) are scarce, this bike could easily have sold for ten times that asking price. So I snapped it up. I threw it in the back of the Zipcar I had rented for the weekend and hauled it back to Boston.

In the end, I spent more money on the new tires and components to turn my bargain find into a single-speed than I did on the actual bike. I called this green-and-black bicycle "Incognito," because of its contrast to my highly recognizable commuter bike. I didn't really need another bike. But I missed the lightness and simplicity of Hideki for just jetting around my neighborhood. The allure of the single-speed bike ensnared me again.

With my new, geared commuter bike for everyday riding, I had a new skill to acquire: shifting. Just about every guide to cycling has a chapter on shifting. In my limited experience, I've learned this skill best by futzing around while riding and observing more experienced cyclists, shifting when they do. As one Olympic mountain biker put it, "The key to proper shifting is thinking ahead," and anticipating where you need to be. You want to shift *before* the terrain changes, not in the middle of it, which also seems like remarkably good advice for being a human.

When you're moving over uneven terrain, shifting is actually what allows you to keep an even cadence. Every cyclist has their own optimal cadence, the frequency of a rotation of the pedals at which they get the most out of their effort. Most city biking doesn't give you much of a chance to find this cadence, with all the starting and stopping you have to do.

Speed up, slow down; speed up, slow down. We do this all the time driving cars, and we think nothing of the extra expense of energy to speed up and slow down between traffic lights. But on a bicycle, you learn quickly what is lost in constantly speeding up and then slamming on the brakes. Because the bike is fueled by your energy, every time you speed up and slow down, you're expending your energy. All the momentum is lost when you come to a screeching halt at every intersection. While keeping an even pace is complicated in the city, the aim is to ride as fluidly as possible.

Consistent cadence is different from consistent speed.

Anyone who has endured a significant challenge can tell you as much—you can keep moving through life at a fast pace, but as the hills become bigger and the trials become greater, the sheer complexity slows you down. An even cadence is hard to acquire, and even harder to maintain. It's a physical and spiritual urban practice I still strive for.

The stories from the monastery kitchen tell of Brother Lawrence's own life cadence: "He worked neither slowly nor hastily, remaining in constant evenness of mind and in unchanging peace." Brother Lawrence knew his cadence, though I have no idea how he learned it. For as much time as I spend on a bike, I still don't seem to know what my default setting is. I aspire to a steady pace. Instead, I seem to start and stop, start and stop, haul ass and fall over.

I've come to love riding behind older male cyclists of a certain variety because of their steady pace. Because these guys have been on the road forever, they've developed an intuitive sense of their own cadence, remaining unfazed when other cyclists blow past them. They're distinctive enough that I'm not the only cyclist who has identified this particular breed.

Bike Snob has given the world the definitive "velo-taxonomy," a kind of field guide to "various subsets of cyclists." You can spot each breed by their plumage: Lycra on roadies, tight black jeans on urban cyclists, and vintage wool sweaters on "Retro-Grouches."

The Retro-Grouch has "passionate respect for the tried and true," hence the abiding devotion to steel over newfangled carbon fiber. Retro-Grouches (otherwise known as Retro-Grumps) are founts of encyclopedic wisdom and, in my experience, have an unfortunate tendency to mansplain to everyone, regardless of gender, exactly how a particular bike component works. Because they're so immersed in these details and committed to old-school componentry, they'll adopt new technology but won't do it for "at least ten to fifteen years to make sure that it *is* better." In New England, we call our particular breed of Retro-Grouches "Freds."

In Boston, Freds ride through every season. In summer, you can identify them unironically wearing old, worn T-shirts, possibly paired with suspenders. In winter, they tend to sport multiple layers of vintage beige or navy-and-beige L. L. Bean sweaters, because if "steel is real," wool is the most trusted cold-weather fabric, better than whatever new-fangled fiber gear is being sold in most bike shops. I've yet to meet a lady Fred.

Somewhat unsurprisingly, given the history of cycling and well, history, misogyny has crept into our velo-vernacular. The smallest chain ring is called the "granny gear" because if you're using it, you're supposedly riding like an old lady or moving at the pace of one. Maybe this is why there aren't any lady Freds; they got tired of being the butt of jokes and left.

But Freds are the real deal. Freds are the guys who were riding in the city before there were bike lanes, before anyone was even thinking or talking about bicycle infrastructure. There's a timelessness to the Freds; they were there before you, and they'll be there after you.

Freds often, but not always, practice the philosophy of "vehicular cycling." During the second cycling boom of the 1970s, a man named John Forester promoted the discipline of vehicular cycling with the notion that "cyclists fare best when they act and are treated as drivers of vehicles." I resist vehicular cycling purists, those who think that if cyclists act like drivers, we'll be treated like drivers. Many women in male-dominated professions have tried this strategy and found that the rules don't apply equally to everyone. I don't think it's a coincidence that the main proponents of vehicular cycling are white men. Acting as if you belong isn't the same as belonging. At best, the system will accommodate you, but it will never fully accept you. The road wasn't built for you. And yet, Freds have an admirable ornery streak as they defiantly travel with cars. I can't ride that way out front, but Freds are good to follow.

Though I don't necessarily want to become a lady Fred, I begrudgingly admire the Freds. They remain steady in adverse conditions; they've seen it all before. The winter of 2014-2015 was historically brutal in Boston. We broke every major snow record. Week after week, the city, including the subway system, was shut down for days at a time. I pride myself on being a four-season cyclist in Boston, but even I had to admit defeat a number of times during the 108.6 inches of snow that fell and buried the city. Curiously, with the subway shut down, bicycles were a dependable way to move around through the snow. The Southwest Corridor bike path wasn't consistently plowed, but the roads were clear-ish. Two-lane roads like Huntington Avenue actually were passable because the piled-up snow reduced the roads to one-and-a-half lanes. Cars could fit in the one lane, and we cyclists took the other half.

I usually avoid Huntington Avenue at all costs. In addition to being a fast road with lots of cars and ambulances heading to the massive campus of hospitals in the Longwood Medical Center, the Green Line MBTA trolley tracks in the middle of the street are a major hazard for cyclists. The deep trolley grooves, which always need to be crossed on the perpendicular, are just the right size to snag a bike wheel. But during this particularly harsh winter, Huntington Avenue to the north and Washington Street to the south became my preferred routes. Through the snow, city residents like me, with a whole lot of grumbling, constantly adapted and reorganized to get where they needed to go.

And through this brutal Boston winter, the Freds led the way out of the darkness—and I know this from personal experience.

Usually the first half of my commute home is on city streets, the second half on the Southwest Corridor bike path. If I want to take a route entirely on city streets like Huntington, I need to decide that almost as soon as I leave my office. During our hellacious winter, the Southwest Corridor bike path was notoriously under-plowed and under-salted, turning what should have been a safe commute home into a wild ride on an ice-skating rink.

One relatively dry evening commute in February 2015, a few days after the most recent snowfall, I decided to follow my usual route and gamble that the Southwest Corridor path was plowed. The roads themselves were fine. I rode down Beacon Hill, shifting into a higher gear and zipping past the cars sitting in traffic. I rode past the Alexander Pope building on Columbus Avenue, steering wide around the cars double-parked in the bike lane. But as soon as I transferred from Columbus onto the Southwest Corridor, I knew I had gambled poorly. The bike path was a sheet of ice.

I was stuck with limited choices. Though this bike path parallels the MBTA Orange Line, it was now rush hour, and bikes weren't allowed on the train. I could lock up my bike and just take the train home, but then I'd be stuck coming back along the same icy path to retrieve it tomorrow. I could also just walk my bike home, but a three-mile trudge through the snow was also unappealing. I could cut down Ruggles Street and pick up Huntington, but that option added both time and distance. So I paused for a moment at the head of the bike path, considering the best of my sub-optimal options.

Just then, from around the corner, a bike pulled up alongside me at the light. He was the only other cyclist I had seen since I left my office. I decided to speak up—maybe he had a solution. "The path looks icy," I said. "Just take it slow," he mumbled from beneath his balaclava, "and follow me." The light changed, and he turned his bushy eyebrows forward, slowly crossing Ruggles Street, using the full "walk" sign to get across. I'm not sure why, but I followed. He seemed to know what he was doing.

He moved at a glacial pace, but still quickly enough to keep his momentum. His wide tires cut a trail in front of me, and I followed, steering my tires into the black grooves. I could tell he knew these roads by heart. He managed to hit every light of every cross street at just the right time to roll on through. No panicked stops, no sharp turns.

"Thanks for the ride," I shouted from behind him as I slowed to turn off the bike path onto Williams Street near my home. He lifted his left hand off the handlebar in just a flash of a wave as he kept going, never turning his head around, not saying another word.

I don't know his name; the only thing I know for sure is that he was a Fred.

I followed him, safely, all the way home. I suspect he rode on to West Roxbury, Hyde Park, or somewhere in that direction further out. I don't know if I've never seen him again, or if I've seen him a thousand times and just haven't noticed. I keep an eye out for that maroon Raleigh and a man with eyebrows like squirrels, but that actually doesn't narrow down the pack of Freds by much.

Wooly, burly, prone to shouting, and a bit lacking in social skills, Freds are the John the Baptists of the cycling world. Before Jesus, John the Baptist hung out in the wilderness, declaring, "I am the voice of one crying out in the wilderness, 'Make straight the way of the Lord.'" John was the forerunner. He saw what was coming before others did, just like the Freds. In their own way, first out on the road, Freds point ahead to the possibility of what bicycle commuting could be. Their urban spiritual practice of keeping a steady pace is a lesson to us all.

It's easy to dismiss Freds as ridiculous caricatures, but they're a valued part of the weird menagerie of cycling characters. Freds move through the city as if it were hospitable, a foretaste of the city to come. John the Baptist also anticipates that future urban vision, a glimpse of the time when "Every valley shall be filled, and every mountain and hill shall be made low, and the crooked shall be made straight, and the rough ways made smooth; and all flesh shall see the salvation of God." We who travel these roads daily long for the crooked to be made straight and the rough ways to be made smooth. With their dependable cadence and their defiant riding in all places and all conditions, Freds point to the possibility of a day when all can ride with the hills made low and the crooked made straight.

Our local patron saint of Freds is Sheldon Brown, of blessed memory. Sheldon was a total original and emblematic of a certain kind of bike nerdery that leads to deeper and deeper plunges into ever-narrower rabbit holes. An employee of Harris Cyclery in Newton, Massachusetts, Sheldon managed an outsized personality and Internet celebrity status. He had an encyclopedic knowledge of bicycles from every era, but especially the odd and obscure. Sheldon is perhaps best known for www.sheldonbrown.com, one of the most trafficked bicycle websites on the Internet with the least amount of polish or corporate backing. The website was first created in 1995, and mostly still looks that way. But it works. It does everything it needs to do, and it's shot through with Sheldon's opinions about every detail of cycling. Sheldon's writings remain intact online, complete with notes and entries added after his death and noted as such, ensuring the reader can distinguish what is authentically the gospel of Sheldon from what is apocryphal. When I want to know how something works or look up a term I don't understand, I go to his website.

The love for Sheldon is near-universal, even among the cycling cynics. Following his death, Bike Snob memorialized him thusly: "As the architect of the cycling canon he's done more for cycling than any pro cyclist, or critical mass, or white bike, or orange bike ever has. No matter what you ride, how you ride, how long you ride, or how long you've been riding, you're a fan of Sheldon Brown."

Around Boston and around the world, dotting the backs of stop signs and bike racks are black-and-white stickers featuring his scraggly beard and proclaiming "Sheldon Brown is my Copilot." I never met Sheldon in person, but then again, most people haven't. Still, he was and is the copilot to many cyclists, a beneficent Fred looking over your shoulder, confidently correcting the thing you're doing wrong. According to his website, he fielded between five hundred and six hundred emails a day. His legacy lives on in his writing and his followers; his wife, Harriet, and his friend John still update his site. Sheldon's *Boston Globe* obituary dubbed him a "cyber-sage."

Sheldon embodied a countercultural witness I love about bicycles: Fix it your own damn self. He wasn't interested in selling you the latest gadget, but offered all the information you'd ever need to make your own repairs. Sheldon's online tutorial on wheel-building is legendary; Abbi learned from Sheldon, and then she taught me. And while they may at times be overbearing, Freds like Sheldon are so passionate about cycling that they can't help sharing their zeal. I love them for wanting to teach others and share the good life on a bike.

John the Baptist and the Freds are out front. The Sweep is at the back.

Those who take on the role of "the Sweep" must practice a Fred-like restraint. My friend Dick Harter has been riding a bike through Cambridge and Boston for longer than I've been alive. The last time we got together for tea, he reminded me that he's been commuting since "before helmets were available." Starting in 1965, Dick commuted from Cambridge to Boston daily until he retired from his law firm in 2012. Now he both rides by himself to get around the city and group-rides in the country. His cycling Rule of Life has become so familiar to him, he says, that "I don't have to think about it, but I'd miss it if it was taken away."

Every Wednesday, Dick rides with a subset of the Charles River Wheelmen known as the "Wednesday Wheelers," mostly a group of retirees and those with flexible schedules. "What binds us together as cyclists," Dick explains, "has replaced the job as our defining structure." On these group rides, Dick often takes up the role of "the Sweep." The Sweep's job is to ride at the back of the pack, ensuring that no rider is lost. Because he's riding in a careful, deliberate way, the Sweep is often pedaling slower than he might otherwise. Dick knows this is a kind of discipline: to intentionally slow down to preserve the group and ensure their safety. "I've spent a lot of my life succeeding because I'm quick," Dick reflects. "I'm not in any way boasting about my new role as the Sweep. I'm here because I'm happy to be here. Riding more slowly on purpose preserves the sense of our community." By sweeping, Dick makes sure that no one is left behind.

I don't know when I'll gain the maturity to ride my own cadence like the Freds or exercise intentional restraint like the Sweeps. I still find myself battling between my desire for a zen-like, even cadence and wanting to go as fast as I can just because I can. Commuting usually feels like an exercise in resisting the temptation to join every race, whether or not I've been invited—and often I haven't been. There will always be cyclists both faster and slower than I am. I wonder what it would be like to ride as if I had nothing to prove.

The Freds and the Sweeps embody a different way to move through the frenetic city, less anxious to make everything a contest and more self-assured in their own cadence. Maybe when I learn to ride like this, at my own pace, I'll have Brother Lawrence's "constant evenness of mind and . . . unchanging peace." This is the urban spiritual discipline that I hope to practice someday. Until then, I have to keep riding to find it.

Chapter 9

Chain | Embodiment

He lifted himself up to God by contemplating the Creation, persuaded that books teach few things in com-
parison with the great book of the world when we know
how to study it as we should. His soul, touched by the
diversity of the parts that make up the world, was lifted
to God so powerfully that nothing was able to separate
it from God.

from Brother Lawrence's Eulogy by the Abbé of Beaufort

114

We mark our bodies as signs of belonging to places. In Boston, a Red Sox hat seems to be the marker that cuts across neighborhood, class, and race. It's not my chosen signifier, but it does seem to be a pretty popular signal for indicating one is "from" Boston (or at least able to purchase something that shows an affinity for Boston).

We also mark our bodies as signs of belonging to ways of life. Many religions have practices of marking the body: Christians smudge their foreheads on Ash Wednesday; Hindus mark their heads and hands with the red-paste *tilaka*. And the Church of Cycling initiates new converts with the chainring tattoo.

This marking easily identifies a bike commuter; it's a physical reminder of how we travel. Cyclists learn to walk the bicycle with the chain-side facing out, but invariably the chain or ring "tattoos" a line of black grease on our legs, pants, or skirts. In theory, the chainring tattoo is the mark of a novice cyclist who should be keeping their chainring clean of the grease and gunk that stains. In reality, we bang around, knocking our bodies and our bikes together. The contact leaves a distinct mark.

There's something vaguely affirming in the chainring tattoo. Moving by car might give us a sore back; walking might give us a blister. But for the most part, our modern transit options don't require much engagement from our physical bodies. Chainring tattoos become the physical reminder that our bodies are involved and invested in our transportation.

Chains hold tension and transfer power. Without chains, modern bicycles wouldn't exist. The "penny farthing" or high-wheelers had direct drive mechanisms: pushing the pedals in the front turned the front wheel. The safety bicycle we know today requires a chain-drive to transfer the motion of the pedals to propel the rear wheel. In fact, without the development of the rolling, linked chain, bikes, cars, and most modern machines wouldn't exist. Chains are a brilliant way to get metal to bend and move.

Chains allow a transfer of power from one location to the next: Legs push pedals, pedals and crank move the chainring, the chainring moves the chain, the chain moves the rear cog, and the cog turns the rear wheel, propelling the bicycle forward. Bikes have rear-wheel drive, as it were. Chains allow for continuous motion instead of the jerking and halting of push and release. For a chain to do its job, it needs sufficient tension. Too loose, and the chain will slip off the gears.

The chain is the mediating mechanism between your movement and the bicycle's movement. But the fundamental experience of the bike remains the same: your body propels it. There's no mechanism or motor moving this bicycle for you.* You are the engine, and your energy drives the bike.

Cycling is a solitary activity done in community; this is as true for a practical bike commuter as it is for a cyclo-cross professional racer. The road-racing cyclists ride in a pace line, taking turns "pulling" the other cyclists in line. Those tucked behind the lead cyclist experience the benefit of about 25 percent less wind resistance. At the same time, a bubble of low-pressure air behind the lead cyclist slightly pushes him or her forward. "Drafting" conserves energy for the group as each cyclist takes his or her turn in the lead. There's a stra-

---

* The major exception here is the "e-bicycle," sometimes known as an "electric" or "e-assist" bicycle. This bike looks like most others, but often has a box containing a motor affixed somewhere along the frame or rack. As "e-bikes" become less the weird, niche toy of Europeans and bike-gadget geeks, a great debate is roaring about whether e-bikes are still bicycles or more like mopeds. I'm more of a purist: I want my bicycle to be entirely human-propelled—"carb-fueled," so to speak. That said, if an e-bike helps me continue to ride in my nineties or if it helps cyclists commute long distances, I'm willing to tolerate it. But strictly speaking, I believe the only kosher bicycle is the one powered by you.

tegic advantage to riding in a group—in terms of both safety and speed—but nobody turns those pedals but you.

There's a certain irony in writing an entire book to encourage people to put down this book and go outside to ride their own bikes. I can tell you how freeing it feels to fly down Beacon Street after a long day, but you'll only fall in love with life on two wheels when the wind is in your own face. I can tell you about the ridiculously joyful moment when, on a rainy ride home, I decided not to spend my time scowling but to aim my wheel at every big puddle I encountered. I can tell you that. But the transformative joy is not yet yours.

I read a lot about spirituality, but at some point, I'm still just reading about other people's experiences of the holy, not experiencing it myself. No doubt I've read lines here and there that somehow articulated the longing that remained unformed in my heart, and thought, *Yes, yes, that must be what God is like.* But I can't read my way to the holy; I have to live my way there.

I'm "drafting" Brother Lawrence—someone who's a bit further ahead, a bit more experienced. This is why we read spiritual guides. We still have to pedal, but the path is a little clearer and the pedaling a little easier.

When I started biking, I read about Boston's best bike routes but soon realized that I would have to ride them to truly know them. Abbi and my friend Trinity taught me how to cut across the Muddy River bike path. Mariana showed me an easier route to the aquarium. Erich pointed out the safest bike lanes in Cambridge. I could pore over maps every day, but I didn't belong to Boston until I biked it. And I couldn't bike it well until others showed me how.

Direct experience is also primary in Brother Lawrence's

spirituality. He doesn't lead us to be more religious in a conventional sense. He's not asking us to spend more time in religious buildings or read more holy books. I hear him coaching us to be more human—not more ethereal, but more grounded. "The great book of the world" is his primary text, and his practice of awareness helps him "study it as we should."

Scripture and church clearly mattered to him. After all, he chose to live in a monastery. But he had a sense of a bigger world, "the great book of the world," and how we should get to know it.

The key to continuous connection, continuous motion, is embodiment. That's what Brother Lawrence believed. The "presence of God" is something we practice to believe. For Brother Lawrence, that practice, that motion, came from having an intimacy with God combined with living embodied in the world: "The good brother found God everywhere, as much in repairing old worn-out shoes as in praying with his community." Like a proto-Nike ad, our shoe-repairing monk believed in the power of "Just do it." Just pray. Just walk. Just chat with God. Just listen. Just peel your potatoes and repair your shoes and listen for God there. Brother Lawrence was less convinced that the practice of the presence of God could be learned in a book.

Faith—and cycling—have a learn-by-doing quality. I practiced riding a bike as a kid, with wise and experienced people teaching me how, with training wheels and a guiding hand at the back of my saddle seat, until I found my balance. It was only then that these teachers gave me a swift push— and only then that I truly began riding on my own. My experience of faith has been similar. The wisdom and guidance of others has helped me find my spiritual balance, but only practice, embodied practice, has brought me into awareness of the transcendent.

The particular Protestant version of Christianity that shaped me is known for its bad habit of disembodiment. At its worst, Protestant Christianity presents our relationship with and worship of the divine as solely an activity from the neck up. Even the most embodied rituals get reduced to anemic versions of what they could be: a sprinkling of water for baptism, crustless white bread for communion.

In working with interfaith gatherings, I've gained a "holy envy" for the traditions that are embodied. My holy envy includes Islam's communal commitment to prayer five times a day, full-bodied prayer that involves bending and kneeling and placing one's head on the earth as a sign of submission to the Creator of the Universe. My envy also includes Judaism's rituals of daily living and "thick," communal Sabbath-keeping. Any tradition that requires baking bread as a religious practice is all right by this carb-fueled velo-practitioner.

I also envy the Jewish prayer books that give structured gratitude for physical things. A few years ago while I was exploring the Buford Highway Farmers Market in Atlanta with my Aunt Barbara, we purchased an unknown fruit. Once we were at home, before cutting through the speckled orange skin to discover what was inside, my aunt, who had converted to Judaism many years ago, recited a prayer: *Barukh'ata Adonai Eloheinu melekh ha'olam borei pri ha'eitz*, which translates into "Blessed are You, Lord our God, Ruler of the Universe, who creates the fruit of the tree." I envy this discipline of gratitude for new things. I've often thought we needed a prayer for the surprise of biking down a previously unknown street, something like, "Blessed are you, God of all Creation, who constantly opens new pathways before us." We are embodied creatures, and we need spiritual practices that reflect our embodiment.

One of the curious side effects of daily biking is the different kind of relationship I've developed with my body. Like most women stewed in the cauldron of American advertising, I've had an uneasy relationship with my body for a very long time. I grew up in the aftermath of Title IX's investment in women's collegiate sports, and the trickle-down effect into girls' athletics. My mom grew up in an era when the only "sport" she could play was cheerleading. Thirty years later, I had the opportunity to be mediocre-to-bad at soccer, gymnastics, ballet, tennis, swimming, volleyball, discus, shot put, field hockey, Irish step-dancing, and rowing. My track record shows me to be an enthusiastic joiner without much proficiency.

Some of my early protestations about biking included repeating "I'm not athletic." In the beginning, I still had the idea that cycling was a competitive sport that required a certain level of athleticism I was sure I didn't have. But peer pressure and the sheer need to get around cheaply without a car overrode my protests. Now, the longer I ride, the more it simply becomes a way of life. Propelling myself through my city has given me both a more embodied spirituality and a profoundly different relationship with my body.

In the beginning, one of the ways I grew in my embodied awareness was by just trying to ride. Practical cycling shouldn't take tons of special gear, I thought. I should just be able to get up and go by bike. But in riding to and from work, what I quickly discovered is that most women's professional clothing isn't designed for movement. We all know this on some level: Just look at a pair of high heels, which are designed for beautiful stillness, not motion. But on the bicycle, I learned this in an embodied way. My clothes fought my body on the bike. Most of the blazers I wore for work were cut too tight for me to reach my arms all the way forward to the handlebars. Most of my shirts were too short in the back as I leaned forward. Most of my shoes weren't designed with a solid enough sole to press hard into the bike pedals. Most of my skirts were cut too narrow to actually allow me to move my legs up and over the top tube of the frame. Skirts that were a perfectly respectable length while I was standing would ride up my thighs while I was biking.

For a while I tried to work within these constraints. My thrift-store work purchases drifted towards A-line skirts with the all-important side pockets so my legs could move. I sought out pants narrower at the hems so the cuffs wouldn't get caught in the bike chain. Still, my struggle continued. Just about every other month someone posts a new trick for women cyclists to modify their existing clothing in order to ride more demurely. Believe me when I say I've tried everything—from tying quarters into the hem of my skirt to keep it weighted in the breeze, to using those clips for the corners of fitted sheets to tether my skirt to my tights, which makes for a home-made and woefully unsexy garter belt. But none of this changes the fundamental problem: women's clothing simply isn't made for movement.

At some point in all this fussing and futzing, I made a decision: Screw it.

I decided I no longer cared about how much thigh I showed while riding. My legs are doing their job. My skirts became the equivalent of the yellow vests of therapy dogs: *These thighs are working. Don't touch and don't comment.* My legs are moving in order to get me where I need to go. Still, I've gotten cat-calls and comments while riding in a skirt. I've even been harassed while riding in January, with every bit of skin except my eyes covered. If even a bicycle burka won't stop other people from lobbing verbal grenades from the safety of their heated cars, then screw it. I'm gonna wear what I want, and everyone's gonna have to deal with it. I've decided this is other people's problem, not mine. Cycling gave me a new understanding of my body, particularly my thighs—not as some flesh that's dangerous to view and needs to be hidden, but as a place of power where my energy comes from.

Because of the bicycle, my clothes changed and my body changed. This is utterly logical and obvious but worth saying: Riding a bike is a physical activity. Part of the reason why I love practical cycling is that I can build an hour of cardio into my day just by biking. True, cycling isn't a comprehensive activity, so cyclists can build up strong legs but still have weak cores and chicken arms. Still, when we ride, our bodies are involved and invested.

The week before Abbi and I got married, I rode my bike to City Hall to pick up the wedding license. Along the way, a car on Washington Street nearly doored me. I slammed on my brakes and stopped in time to avoid getting clipped by the driver's side door. But I had a hard time unclipping my foot from the pedal, and my bike listed to the right, the chainring digging into my shin. Conveniently, my wedding dress was long enough to cover up the chainring-shaped scab on my leg. I got married with something old, something new, something borrowed, and something that reminds me that my body can move me powerfully and independently through my city.

That wound—I knew where it came from. But the origin of others isn't so clear. One of the strange consequences of regular bike-riding is the appearance of mysterious bruises on my body—nothing too painful, just surface marks of my travel. Clipping my hip as I carry the bike up the stairs from the basement, or thwapping my hand as I fiddle with a bungee cord—the resulting bruises serve as odd badges of honor, a reminder of my embodiment and the physicality of my movement.

Dead skin doesn't bruise—only living flesh does. So bicycle bruises are signs of life. I think this is why cyclo-cross racers love to talk about (and post photos of) their wounds: these markings signify life.

Cycling promises an embodied knowledge, but not without some mortification of the flesh. You're gonna fall. You're gonna bruise. You're making the decision to travel on the road unprotected by a giant metal shell. Cycling is the embodied decision to make yourself vulnerable in order that you might move more freely.

After five years of riding through all four of Boston's dramatically different seasons, I've gained an embodied knowledge of the weather. I know what a difference it makes when there's a wind at my back. I know I can ride in the rain and not melt. I know the playfulness of riding through a summer storm, the pavement still so hot that steam rises up as the rain hits the ground.

I now know the temperature intuitively. I know the difference between riding bare-handed at forty-one degrees and wanting gloves at thirty-six degrees after the sun has gone down. I know that if I walk out the door to ride and I'm comfortable with the temperature, I'm wearing too many layers. Cyclists warm up as we ride, so it's best to start out cold, but not too cold. My lower temperature limit for biking in winter is around eighteen degrees, though Abbi has figured out how to go even lower with mountaineering gloves on her hands and chemical heating pads in her bike shoes.

I now also know that I stay happier through the long winter when I actually spend some time outside in the limited winter sunlight. It's tempting to hibernate indoors through Boston's interminable winters. But commuting by bike gets me outside when the days are short and the wind is fierce. Even that little bit of sun and bracing wind helps me feel alive.

I fear this is starting to sound like the evangelical zeal of a late-night infomercial: I stay healthier, I remain happier, all because of this magical bicycle pill! But I didn't know these things about the environment around me—or I didn't know these things in an embodied way—from inside a car or the subway.

Now I know the feeling of freedom in my body, the good, hard work of pushing up a hill and the rush of flying back down the other side. I know in my bones the split-second experience of feeling like I might just defy the earth's gravitational pull. I know in the moments when my legs can hardly keep up that I'm not thinking of all that weighs me down and binds me. Instead, for an increasingly middle-aged and un-athletic woman, I'm feeling strong and powerful and free on my bike. There has to be something true of the transcendent and the holy in that experience.

My time in the saddle mirrors my soul's relationship with God: rolling joy at finding myself on a previously un-ridden street, and startling anxiety as something unknown threatens my path. And when I really get riding, when I really get in my groove, I can drift into Brother Lawrence's "silent, secret, nearly unbroken conversation of the soul with God." I know for sure I never found this conversation sitting on my couch, reading a book on my own. Instead, I've stumbled on it in the embodied spiritual practice of riding my bike along the city's roads.

Chapter 10

Helmet | Particularity

Even though by nature he had a great aversion to doing kitchen work, he became accustomed to doing everything there out of love for God, and asked God in every situation for grace to do his work. So he found that kitchen work became easy for him during the fifteen years he was assigned there.

The Abbé of Beaufort on Conversation with Brother Lawrence,
September 8, 1666

Cyclists are opinionated people—and I'm one of them. Since I refuse to let this chapter get sucked into a never-ending flame war about helmets, I'm putting my cards on the table upfront: I believe that it's safer and smarter to ride a bike in America wearing a helmet, but I don't believe in legislating adults to do so.

I understand the disdain. Helmets are neither the most freeing nor flattering of accessories. When I imagine bicycle utopia, my hair is blowing in the breeze, not smushed under a helmet. Just as Brother Lawrence acknowledged his initial discomfort in the monastery kitchen, I need to acknowledge cyclists' collective aversion to helmets while I make my own personal peace with the giant plastic bowl on my head.

Questions over adequate head protection have been around as long as there have been bicycles. We have the high-wheeler to thank for the term "header" or "taking a header," because on this bike the unfortunate cyclist would somersault over the giant wheel and land on the ground. The earliest "helmets" were really more like padded hats, with strips of leather covering bands of wool padding. According to an oral history of bicycle helmets, these "hairnets" did a better job of keeping one's ears intact when skidding along the road than absorbing impact.

With the second great bike boom of the 1970s, some cyclists started to borrow hockey and mountain-climbing helmets in the absence of any national bicycle-helmet standards. Eventually, materials development in foams and plastics allowed for the creation of modern helmets, with wide variations and improvements in size, shape, thickness, exterior shell, and ventilation. And most sane cyclists will acknowledge that "bicycle helmets provide significant protection against . . . [head] . . . injuries, but they are no magic bullet."

Even though most cycling deaths involve riders not wearing helmets, questions of correlation and causation abound.

Did they die because they weren't wearing helmets when they crashed, or were they more likely to crash because cyclists who ride helmet-less are a less cautious subset of cyclists to begin with?

Making helmets mandatory adds another barrier to riding bicycles because helmets aren't universally accessible, either for those using city-based bike-share systems or for all classes of bicycle riders. The neighborhoods where folks are riding bikes out of necessity aren't exactly flush with bike shops selling helmets.

And how do helmet laws affect the popularity of cycling? Mandatory helmet laws in parts of Australia, New Zealand, and Canada "did seem to reduce cycling." Policy wonks wonder: Do mandatory helmet laws give the impression that cycling is a dangerous activity? Is riding a bike actually any more dangerous than driving a car? Urban cyclist Robert Hurst, who reviewed several studies, writes, "Statistically, an hour of driving is almost twice as deadly as an hour of cycling, and it is at least as likely to cause a serious head injury." If moving through the city is really so dangerous on the whole, should we require all pedestrians and motorists to wear helmets too?

There's a particular kind of helmet-shaming that happens after a crash, even when it's unclear if the helmet would have protected the cyclist against the consequences. (Lord knows my helmet didn't protect my back when I was hit by a car, though I'm still glad I was wearing one.) You can find this helmet-shaming mantra dependably in the comment sections of every news story involving bicycles. "Should have worn a helmet" is the usual victim-blaming rendered. We tend to treat crashes as solely the product of individual actions, not systemic consequences of an unequal transit system primed for conflict.

My unscientific assessment is that cyclists generally come around to helmets even if they don't start there. Ride in the city long enough, and you develop an awareness of all the ways you could be hurt by someone else's negligence. After that, it's a short trip to thinking, *Hey—why don't I just take an extra precaution, like wearing a helmet?*

Cyclists have a clear awareness of our vulnerability as humans in transit—a vulnerability that a car obscures for most drivers. We know that we're exposed to the elements. We know that our safety depends not just on our own skill and visibility, but also on the drivers and the consideration of those around us on the road. This is more than a logical awareness—it's a spiritual awareness: our safety is not entirely within our control. We can put on helmets to minimize the damage, but at the end of the day, we're at the mercy of those around us.

Ultimately, though, 95 percent of all the statistics can be used to justify any position you want to take in the helmet debate. I realize that—and I'm both unqualified to sort this out and uninterested in doing it. What I'm most interested in is thinking about how helmets often serve as icons of our urban anonymity.

Anonymity is a defining characteristic of cities. The sheer volume of people makes it hard to be known in every place. Some of us crave or even seek out this urban anonymity because it may afford a certain kind of peacefulness, a solitary experience in a crowd. We're surrounded by thousands of other people, and yet we're alone, sitting in the library, moving down the sidewalk, waiting in the back of a sanctuary. Many a story is based on the trope of leaving behind one's former small-town self and reinventing oneself in the big city. The city holds out the possibility of escaping the sometimes-claustrophobic familiarity of a small town and moving freely. And helmets add a layer of further anonymity in the city. (Mind you, sitting in a metal box hermetically sealed off from the rest of the city is actually a thicker layer of urban anonymity.)

But something about this urban anonymity also allows us to dehumanize one another. I think, at a more subconscious level, the ubiquitous "baby on board" car signs of the mid-1980s and the stick-figure family-car decals of the past decade function as ways to undercut the anonymity of the road. Those signs attempt to remind others that there are particular human beings inside those vehicles. And yet too many of us drive in an anonymous and dehumanizing way.

On the road, sealed in our vehicles, we shout at one another and behave in ways we never would at the post office or the grocery store. We think of the road as a means to an end, the necessary evil for getting to the place we want to be. Many cyclists know the road itself is part of the journey and can also be part of the joy. I'd venture to say that if you're an aggressive driver who's making life dangerous for cyclists and scaring pedestrians because you're running late on your way to feed poor people, then you're not adding as much goodness to the world as you could. How we travel through life—not just where we end up—matters.

If cities form us by daily experiences of anonymity, the correlative urban spiritual discipline is to be seen and known in our particularity. My distinctive bicycle helps me to be seen and known by my neighbors. Slowing down enough to say "Hello" breaks the anonymity just a bit. But more than anything, the regularity of my bike route reduces the undifferentiated crowds of the city into a daily pattern of particularity: I see the same shop owners opening up in Egleston Square, the same construction workers demolishing an abandoned bus depot turned into a street-art venue called Bartlett Yard, the same city workers filing into the Boston Public School building in Dudley Square, the same crossing guard in front of the Josiah Quincy Elementary School in Chinatown. The daily habit of moving through the city along the same route, as others move along their usual routes, focuses the city from unknown and anonymous to known and particular.

I think Brother Lawrence would tell us that to be seen and known in our particularity, we need to be in intimate and perpetual conversation with God, the same sort of regularity of habit that gets us to know our neighbors. How can God get to know us if we don't listen and talk regularly? For Brother Lawrence, the continual conversation begins by recognizing "God's intimate presence within us" and then speaking "to Him every moment, asking Him for His help."

To love our neighbors as ourselves, we've got to know what it looks like to love ourselves, in all our particularity. In some ways, I think it may be easier for us to be known in our particularity by God than by one another. Despite daily routes and usual characters, the anonymity of the city is a hard thing to overcome.

That's where helmets can help in a distinctive way. At the same time that helmets insulate us and make us anonymous, they are also visible markers of a particular species. With helmets on our heads, we're marked as cyclists.

There's a cyclist in Boston who is readily identifiable by his helmet. I don't know his name, and he's much faster than I am, so I rarely ride with him for very long, but I recognize him because he's got a bird perched on top of his head. From a distance, it's totally unclear how this bird ended up on top of his head and how it stays there. But close up, the mystery vanishes. I know this because once I pulled up behind him at an intersection and clearly saw the top of his helmet—where he's affixed what appears to be a stuffed pigeon. I have no idea why he decorated his helmet this way, but I can guess at what he's seeking. In the undifferentiated masses of the city, he is immediately recognizable.

I've come to take every one of these helmet bird-sightings as a visible reminder that, in the words of the gospel song, "His eye is on the sparrow, and I know He watches me." The challenge of a robust urban spirituality is not only to know that God's eye is on me, but to see every anonymous person in this city as a particular and worthy human. And like Brother Lawrence peeling potatoes in the monastery kitchen, I realize that the longer I ride in the city, the more I recognize the particularity and thus the holiness around me.

The road has become a thick metaphor for me in thinking about how I move through life in my own particularity. I've obeyed most of the rules, most of my life, following well-worn paths to social mobility and social respectability, even before I could have articulated that as what I was doing. Recently, when I was riding home late at night from a movie with my friend Marisa, the roads were almost totally clear. At the intersection where the Southwest Corridor crosses over Centre Street at Jackson Square, Marisa ran the notoriously long red light across empty lanes of traffic. She waited patiently on the other side, until the light changed and I rolled across. "There isn't a car for a mile!" Marisa exclaimed. "You could have crossed." I could have, but my thorough conditioning to follow the rules runs deep. I've drunk the insidious mythology that following each and every rule will keep me safe and inoffensive. But striving to be inoffensive is not a noble ethic for living.

Riding a bicycle through the city has taught me that even obeying every single rule won't guarantee my safety or shield me from criticism. I can behave as well as I can actively muster, and still, some drivers will call me horrible names and possibly threaten my life even when I have the right of way. There's nothing—no helmet or way of being—that can protect me from that.

Others have found the rich metaphor of the road to be a generative way to understand how people are treated differently. They have seen how roadways privilege some users and disempower others. Blogger and cyclist Jeremy Dowsett stirred up many in the summer of 2014 when he wrote a widely shared blog post: "What My Bike Taught Me about White Privilege." Dowsett had been commuting for the past five years in Lansing, Michigan, deep in the heart of American car culture. Dowsett wrote, "I can imagine that for people of color, life in a white-majority context feels a bit like being on a bicycle in the midst of traffic. They have the right to be on the road, and laws on the books to make it equitable, but that doesn't change the fact that they are on a bike in a world made for cars."

His post was an attempt to move conversations about white privilege from the personal to the systemic, to shine a light on what can be invisible to the privileged: an entire system designed for their benefit. In a follow-up post, Dowsett acknowledged the limits of the road metaphor: "The experience I [as a white man] have as a cyclist—the disproportionate sense of power, the inequality of our road system, the fear of getting squashed—those all disappear for me when I get off my bike. For people of color, however, there's no getting off the bike." The longer I ride through this city with a more diverse community, the more I have come to see that for particular fellow cyclists, there's no getting off inhospitable roads.

I had obeyed most of the (implicit) rules as a respectable, upper-middle-class white Christian woman—until I decided to marry Abbi. When we made public the news of our intention to marry, many people were accepting and kind. Others ranged from disappointed to angry. I had broken the code of inoffensiveness. I had become particular in a way some people didn't like.

It's a very strange thing to feel that your very existence is offensive or anger-inducing to some people. Cycling through the city for a number of years had made me realize that my very existence provokes anger in some people—but I wasn't prepared for this particular response. Maybe because she's been on the road for more years than I have, Abbi just let the negative comments about our marriage roll off her back. But they wounded me. They kept me up at night. The anonymous commentary was a sort of road rash, broad and surface-level, and quick to dissipate. But the people I knew and loved who were hurt or disappointed by our decision to marry—that was the gravel stuck under my skin. Despite my years spent riding through the city, I have not yet mastered the spiritual discipline of non-reactivity.

Cyclists experience another kind of particularity—what I've come to understand as the anger paradox of the road. We go to the (inhospitable) road to work out our own tensions, but on that road we're confronted by the anger of motorists directed at us. I know without a doubt that a long ride after a stressful day at the office is a near-certain way for me to work out my anger and irritation. But I also know that my blood pressure rises after the third driver in a row has nearly killed me on my commute home.

Living in and moving through an inhospitable space take their toll. We cyclists guard and buffer ourselves as best we can. We affix bright lights to our bikes, and wear reflective clothing, and put helmets on our heads. In the event of a crash, the smooth, hard plastic exterior is designed to slide across the pavement rather than get stuck; the foam interior is designed to absorb impact. But there's only so much a helmet can do. The habit of cycling means that we are exposed to and absorb a lot. We are exposed to and inhale all the fumes of vehicles burning fuel around us. We are exposed to and feel the climate change in our bodies. We are exposed to and absorb other people's anger. What does this do to us, and what should our response be?

I am unsure that peaceful non-violence actually is the right response.

I know what I *should* say as a Christian, as someone who is trying to live peacefully and non-violently in the world. But I also know what I experience as a cyclist, day in and day out. I know the layers of anger that build up like road grit from the daily experience of being treated as less than human, as expendable, as anonymous.

I am genuinely unsure how to think about anger and bicycles, and if non-reactivity is the right response. When I was chatting with the mechanics at Hub Bicycle, we traded tales of the indignities visited upon us by drivers acting like they owned the road. Every urban cyclist has experienced the sheer ignorance of our fellow commuters regarding the legalities of road usage. And most roadways seem designed not for peaceful co-existence, but conflict.

When we enter an inhospitable road, motorists shout at us to get on the sidewalk (which is illegal in most commercial and many residential areas). Should we get on the sidewalk (illegally), pedestrians will (rightly) demand that we get out of their way and move onto the road. Should we get back on the road, some motorist has probably decided to double-park in the painted bike lane, forcing us into the flow of car traffic. Almost as soon as we move into that flow, a motorist shouts at us to get back into the bike lane. It's easy to understand how we cyclists develop a chip on our shoulders about being a particular and persecuted transit minority that no one else wants around.

Then again, we tend to tell stories of road rage in which we are the spotless heroes. As a preacher, I know that one of the truisms of our craft is "never become the hero of your own sermon." In our cycling stories, everyone else is thoughtless at best and murderous at worst, and our behavior is flawless. I admit it—I'm not always a perfect driver. I speed; I've rolled through stop signs; I've failed to yield. I'm not always the perfect pedestrian, either. I've been known to step off the curb as the light is already flashing and cross in the middle of the road. And I'm not always the perfect cyclist. My list of biking infractions is long. In one of the prayers of confession in the Episcopal Book of Common Prayer, the penitent confesses "what I have done, and what I have left undone." There's plenty I've done and left undone on the road.

After confessing the done and the undone, this particular prayer of confession continues, "We have not loved you with our whole heart; we have not loved our neighbors as ourselves." To me, this is the crux of the shared space of the road and, at a larger level, of the city: How do we "love our neighbor" as ourselves? How do we live in a way that makes real the equal dignity and equal humanity of each and every person, both the ones we know and those rendered anonymous? How do we move through the city in our various ways, all the while acknowledging that some of us have more protection and some of us wield more power to injure and harm on a road that we claim is for all but that privileges some?

We speak in ways that make our fellow neighbors anonymous and dehumanized—"that car" or "that bike" rather than "that motorist" or "that cyclist," or even "that person driving a car," or "that person riding a bike." It's a lethal combination—the anonymity of cities, combined with the anxiety of transit, mixed with the competitiveness of the road. If we don't treat every other traveler with particularity and equal dignity, someone will end up dead.

How do you treat your neighbor with equal dignity when you believe your neighbor's actions are either negligent or malicious?

I tossed this idea around with other cyclists while hanging out again at Hub Bicycle. Emily responded, "Anger is not the right response to negligence."

I think she's right, but what is? Education? Consciousness-raising?

I know what I want to be: kind, generous, and gracious. But what I feel is resentful, expendable, and angry. I want to be seen. I want to be treated as a particular human, not just an anonymous nuisance in the way of an anonymous driver getting to the next red light.

How do I see the full and particular humanity of the negligent truck driver who nearly right-hooked me? How do I cultivate the moral imagination to wonder how many hours he had been driving for a paycheck that barely pays the rent? How do I imagine how tired he's feeling after fourteen hours already on the road? Can I sympathize with his anger and anxiety over being stuck in traffic when he's supposed to deliver his truck in the next fifteen minutes? Can I look beyond the anonymity of the road through the windshield dimly to see this driver who's threatening my life as another human being?

I want to. But I'm not there yet.

Chapter 11

Brakes | Limitations

We cannot avoid the dangers and reefs that life holds without the very present help of God. Let us ask God continually for it. How can we ask for it unless we are with God? How can we think often about God except through the holy practice that we must form within ourselves? You will probably tell me that I am always telling you the same thing. That is true!

Letter "To the Reverend Mother N . . ."
from Brother Lawrence, March 28, 1689

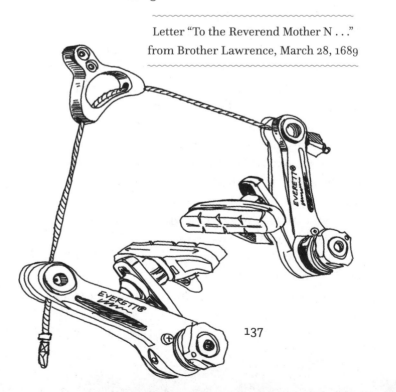

137

Brother Lawrence is right: We cannot avoid the dangers. We can only learn how to steer and brake.

The invention of bicycles allowed human-powered movement four to five times more efficient than that of our feet. Yet, ever since the first bike was created, we've been trying to figure out the best way to stop it. Going far and fast is only useful if you can also stop on command.

The earliest bicycles employed a range of inferior stopping options, including spoon brakes and rod brakes—and simply putting one's feet on the ground. In the most basic of terms, stopping is possible because of friction. But to be truly useful, the early bicycle needed a more precise mode of braking than just running up a hill and grinding to a halt.

Today, bike brakes have been radically improved. Except for a few oddities, there are three main types of brakes: coaster, rim, and disc. Coaster brakes cause the rear wheel to stop moving when the cyclist pushes backwards on the pedals. Rim brakes apply pressure to both sides of the rim of both wheels, and the pressure between the rim and the brake shoe causes the wheel to stop moving. Disc brakes affix a metal disc alongside the wheel near the hub, and this provides the point of contact for friction and stopping.

Most bikes have two sets of brakes, one in the front and one in the rear, an intentional redundancy so that if one set fails, the other is available. Additionally, the combined use of front and rear brakes allows more controlled riding and stopping. Use just the front brake in a moment of crisis, and chances are your bike will stop, but you may keep going—over the handlebars.

Braking is about control and boundaries. Skilled city cyclists aim to ride in such a way that we're not constantly slamming into other people, vehicles, or inanimate objects. Or, as Robert Hurst puts it in *The Art of Urban Cycling*, "Panic stops are a symptom of cyclists' mistakes." Sometimes, of course, other travelers violate our boundaries and force us to make panic stops. But the goal is to move and stop in such a way that our stopping is by design, not accident.

While Hurst teaches how to "panic stop," he still counsels, "It is better to anticipate problems well ahead of time and to avoid situations where problems elude anticipation." Hurst wants cyclists to focus on avoiding the dangers. Brother Lawrence tacks in a slightly different direction, claiming we cannot avoid the dangers of life. I think I'm somewhere in between. My goal is to ride with a margin for error—both my own and that of drivers around me. In order to avoid panic stops, I aim to ride aware of the possible perils surrounding me. Brother Lawrence's quick answer to this condition is constant awareness of "the very present help of God." This heightened awareness of an ever-present God allowed him to travel through life with the capacity to both brake and steer.

Spiritually mature cycling means knowing our boundaries and seeking to ride within our limits. Of course we can press that outer edge of our limitations, trying to ride harder, faster, longer, in a more technically complex way than we have before. But when and where we press these limitations—and how and why we choose to do that—are critical matters if we want to develop a mature urban practice of respecting boundaries.

Boundaries define cities as well as people. In Boston, some of the neighborhoods have geographic features that define their borders, like the Charles River to Allston's north, or Dorchester Bay to South Boston's east. Other Boston neighborhoods developed new boundaries when they were annexed, such as Roxbury and Hyde Park.

We tend to think of cities as only moving in an expansive

direction, when the opposite is true as well. Riding the whale-oil boom, New Bedford, Massachusetts, was the richest city per capita in the world in the mid-1800s, but now it struggles with a decreasing population and fewer economic opportunities for the residents that remain. The city of Detroit, once proud and powerful, has endured decades of struggle, population loss, and a bankrupt municipal government. Now some are asking if Detroit ought to contract geographically as its population continues to shrink.

There is no standard global definition for what constitutes a city, but all cities are bound in various ways. We can categorize cities by demographics, considering their geographic size and their population density. We can categorize cities by their functions, observing that they behave as hubs for commercial, political, and even religious functions for a broader geographic area. We can also categorize cities as places where residents can be bound together by a shared experience of place. But however we define a city, there are boundaries. Some things are in, and some things are out.

One theory of urban development holds that the location of cities is partially determined by a desire to protect and defend. If dangers can't be avoided, then the city must have certain clear, identifiable boundaries to defend. Ancient walled cities bear out this theory, but so do places like Boston. We are a city positioned for defense. Castle Island in South Boston has served as a fortification since 1634. A Revolutionary War lookout tower sits high up Prospect Hill in Somerville, giving the city a vantage point from which to detect arriving aggressors. The western border is relatively unprotected. I guess our colonial forebears didn't think the (now-fancy) suburb of Newton was about to rise up and attack.

Colloquially, you can hear how boundaries of cities are reinforced in conversations about where people are from or where they live. "The New York City area" accurately describes where I grew up, but those boundaries are too expansive for most New York City residents. Derisively, we New Jerseyans were called "BNT" or "Bridge and Tunnel," a slam on how we needed to cross those borders to enter New York City. "Metro Boston" is a fine definition of our region but not a terribly precise designation if you're talking with someone who is "OFD," or "Originally from Dorchester." Cities have boundaries; neighborhoods certainly do.

The boundedness of cities is not necessarily a bad thing. At one extreme, a city like Houston, with tremendous urban sprawl spreading people and places far apart, makes moving in-between difficult. At the other extreme, a tightly bounded city like the walled Old City of Jerusalem is so constrained by space that the compression of people into cramped quarters feels like it increases the tension. Such extremes make me wonder: In large cities like Los Angeles, which covers nearly ten times more square miles than Boston, is it possible to have a shared experience of being *from* the same city?

The more I travel across the neighborhood boundaries of this city, the more I believe that even in compact Boston, we don't share a common experience. And that was most apparent after the Boston Marathon bombings. Despite our "Boston Strong" bond, the distance between the experience of downtown and that of other neighborhoods was vividly on display.

On a Friday night in April 2014, almost a year after the bombings, I rode my bike toward Dudley Square. I coasted down Washington Street and, instead of continuing towards downtown, took a right onto Martin Luther King Jr. Boulevard, then a left onto Warren Street, securing my bike in front of St. John's Missionary Baptist Church.

Inside, we gathered, mostly folks from Boston's neighborhoods further out from the center of the city. In a few days, the elected leaders and clergy and first responders and dignitaries would gather downtown to mark the first anniversary of the bombings. But Boston's black clergy had organized this additional prayer service before that. The Boston Marathon bombings and aftermath left six people dead and 264 injured. But in the year that followed, 235 people had been shot in Boston, with thirty-five people senselessly killed. For these thirty-five and their families, there were no T-shirts or slogans, no visiting celebrities, no "One Fund." At that church in Roxbury, after the prayers and the singing, we passed the collection plate so that a mother could afford to bury her murdered son.

In the immediate aftermath of the collective trauma of both the bombings and a manhunt, Bostonians and then the nation rallied around the cry "One Boston." But we were not as bound together as the slogan claimed. There were entire neighborhoods in the city whose suffering was considered unremarkable, and therefore unseen. While many claimed we were "Boston Strong," not everyone felt that way. To live together well in cities with complex histories and bounded neighborhoods, we need the humility to recognize our own boundedness. What I experience living in Jamaica Plain is different from the experience of a person living in Brighton or Mission Hill or Hyde Park.

In the wake of those two different prayer services, the one in Roxbury and the one downtown, I have intentionally become much more cautious about speaking of our city as though it were a coherent, shared experience for every Bostonian. In those pews I was chastened to remember the limits of my own experience. There are many Bostons. My usual route is just one path among many through this city.

Again and again on our city streets, cycling challenges me to know my limitations, to know when to put on the brakes.

Perhaps the biggest temptation for me to blow through my own boundaries comes in a particularly seductive experience known as "the commuter race." I start out with a steady pace on a pleasant ride home, but then some knucklehead scorches past me without a warning and then shoots through a stop sign. Just like that, the spark ignites, and I feel an overwhelming need to prove that I'm just as fast. All of a sudden, a leisurely commute has become a turn at the velodrome.

I grew up with a healthy sense of competition. In my family we learned young to play hard and to win. At one level, commuter races are utterly harmless. Cyclists have to get to and from certain locations, so why not have some fun doing it? At another level, I feel compelled to prove myself as a cyclist. For some awful reason, I feel like my honor has been impugned when another cyclist presumes he or she is faster than I am.

That cyclists succumb to races is no wonder. We've made the entire road into a racetrack. The problem comes when the commuter race takes on the weight of a battle between good and evil, or defending one's honor as a cyclist. This is nuts. The way of wisdom is not to compete in every race to which you're invited, because not every race is worthwhile. Pushing harder and faster isn't always the height of cycling spiritual maturity.

I've pushed other limits on a bike that have left me by the side of the road a chastened, weepy mess. On an annual retreat with colleagues in Boone, North Carolina, I took the afternoon break to borrow a road bike and ride a stretch of the Blue Ridge Parkway. A free afternoon and a famous roadway were just too tempting. Never mind that I'm not a big road cyclist, or that I was riding a completely unfamiliar bike and adventuring on an unknown stretch of road.

Most of my hours in the saddle are spent on flat city roads, not mountainous terrain. But I was seduced by an iconic parkway known for its stunning vistas. How could I be so close to this much beauty and not try to ride it?

I learned the hard way that I wasn't experienced enough to cycle these roads. The hills were steeper than anything I had ridden before—and if uphill was frustrating, downhill was traumatic. It was a miserable roller-coaster combination of picking up too much speed on the downhill and then trying to ride that momentum up the next hill. Soon I crested one ridge only to see the road drop in front of me, but I had neither enough time nor enough wisdom to stop. I rode the brakes all the way down into the valley, braking so hard that my hands cramped up on the handlebars. I finally came to a stop at the lowest point between two hills.

My hands were still stinging as I got off the bike and sat down by the side of the road to pull myself back together. The lesson was clear: The hills were more than I could handle, and the bike was more than I could control. Cars sped past as the bike and I cowered by the roadside. In that moment, there was nothing transcendent. My thoughts were not about the God of all Creation who would line up mountain after mountain in cascades of blue just to give me the pleasure of gazing upon their beauty. Instead, I was massaging the cramps out of my hands, cursing my own stupidity, and wondering how I was going to get off this damn hill.

It is said of Brother Lawrence, "When he failed, he did nothing but admit his fault and say to God, 'I will never do anything else if you leave me alone; it is up to you to prevent me from falling and to correct what is not good.' Afterward, he did not trouble himself at all about his fault." I admired his mature spiritual practice, but I couldn't follow his example. Even after I got down off the mountain alive, returned the bike, and skulked back to my friends, all the while vowing not to ride in places for which I was unprepared, I was still troubling myself about my faults. All those cars passed me by, a humiliated puddle of a novice cyclist on the side of the road. I spent a perfectly good, free afternoon—something rare—intentionally putting myself in a situation far beyond my capabilities. Why couldn't I have acknowledged my limitations and taken a walk instead, or at most a ride through town?

When you ride, road grit is the residual stuff that sticks with you. It builds up. Yes, I was fine, and the bike was fine. No permanent damage done. And no catastrophic problem like a nail in the tire. But I could feel the existential grit, and unlike Brother Lawrence, I couldn't help but be troubled by it.

Unless you remove the grit, it will wear you down. On a bike, you want enough friction to allow you to stop, but not so much that you're grinding through your brake pads. And any bike that does more than serve as a laundry rack and actually makes it outside needs to be cleaned regularly. Like everything else, it has its strengths—and its limitations.

Cycling has its own rhythms and rituals, a set of disciplines necessary to ride well. There are the daily rituals: Check the air in the tires. Check to make sure the chain is properly greased. Check that you've got a helmet, lights, and a lock. And then there are seasonal rituals: a spring check-up before the faster rides of warmer weather; maybe a mid-summer tune-up; a fall scrub-down to remove all that summer mud; and a winter deep-clean to wipe away the road salt before it starts to corrode the metal.

For me, these regular overhauls and deep cleans of my bike are the mechanical equivalent of going on spiritual retreats. I've been going on silent, overnight retreats now for about twelve years. I followed a more predictable rhythm while in school: one retreat during the fall semester, one during the spring. Since I've been working, my rhythm has been more erratic. Most often, I've worked too much, come to a screeching halt in the depths of the valley of my life, and realized I haven't respected my limitations. Then I've called up the monastery with a desperate plea: "How soon can I come and stay with you?" The brothers of the Society of St. John the Evangelist provide a place of refuge for me and for many.

Just a few days away on silent retreat give me the time and space to clean off all the grit I've accumulated just moving through the world. I'm not entirely sure how, and I'm not entirely sure why, but hiding out in a monastery for a couple of days gives me the feeling of being overhauled. Maybe it's having someone else in charge: I don't have to make many decisions on retreat. And someone else is setting the limits. The brothers have a set schedule of prayers and meals; I just follow along at the back of the pack. I can't race ahead. At first it was scary for me to imagine—let alone embrace—not talking for a few days. Now I appreciate the silence and shedding the obligation to make small talk. We talk when it's necessary, but there's no extraneous chatting. The silence allows me to restart some of those conversations with God that got dropped as I was racing through my life.

I've stayed at both the rural and the urban guesthouses of the Society of St. John the Evangelist. At their monastic farmhouse near the New Hampshire border, the loudest noise comes from the chickens. It's hard to see the nearest neighbor. The deep sense of stillness I feel there is partly from the place itself. But at the monastery in the city of Cambridge, I can still hear the ambulances on Memorial Drive.

From inside, I can hear the impatient cars during rush hour. From a number of the guest rooms, I can see the apartment building next door. And yet, within the bounds of the thick stone walls, as the brothers quietly scuff their sandals along the marble floor and use words with judicious spareness, I can find stillness, too.

It's not the retreat to the rural that saves me, but the momentary stepping out of the race. I've almost entirely and uncritically adopted the metaphor of life as a race—and the toxic consequences that come with it. If life is a race, then everything is a competition. If life is a race, then everyone is competing against me. If life is a race, then some will win, but many more will lose. If life is a race, then the fastest, not the kindest, is the victor.

Do most of us think of daily life as a race? If we do, then we've unconsciously adopted a "Sports Utility Vehicle theology," in the words of Carol Johnston, where we attempt to buy our way to security, where the strongest survive and the vulnerable are left to fend for themselves, where bigger is better at the expense of everyone else around us. And if life is a race, we're reluctant to pull over and leave the road for a bit to repair and overhaul.

This is not how I want to live. I want to develop urban spiritual practices that honor how I travel, that shore up my soul, that respect both my limits and those of others.

After that hard, honest prayer service in Roxbury, I biked home in silence. Instead of retracing my route, I wandered by bike towards home. Back down Warren Street, left onto MLK Boulevard, but this time cutting up Walnut Street. Off the fast main roads and into the slower streets of the neighborhoods. I needed to absorb all I had heard. I put my cell-phone map away and just rode, trusting that I knew these streets well enough by now to guide myself home.

The metaphor of the road is thick with possibilities: a road that meanders, dead-ends, forces us to turn, offers options, and guides us somewhere surprising. My route home that night was a ride, not a race.

Chapter 12

You | Joy

We do not have to be constantly at church to be with God. We can make our hearts a prayer room into which we can retire from time to time to converse with God, gently, humbly, and lovingly. Everyone is capable of these familiar conversations with God—some more, some less.

Fourth Letter, "To Madame N . . ."
from Brother Lawrence, undated

However, we must always continue to labor, since in the life of the spirit, not to advance is to fall back. But those who have the wind of the Holy Spirit sail even while they sleep. If the skiff of our soul is still battered by winds or by tempests, let us awaken the Lord who is resting there. God will soon calm the sea.

First Letter, "To the Reverend Mother N . . ."
from Brother Lawrence, Paris, 1682

You may have the slickest gear, the lightest frame, and the fanciest wheels in the whole world, but that glorious bike will not move without *you*. In the end, the most unique, most irreplaceable, and holiest part of the bicycle is you.

The rider matters more than the bike. My bicycle guides me down some surprising roads and has given me some unexpected gifts: stronger legs, dearer neighbors, more creative curse words, and a practice of the presence of God. Over all these roads, with every turn of the pedal, grows my awareness that I am integral to the practice.

You, the rider, are the most important part of the bike. The particulars of who you are and where you've been are critical to how you move through the world. Like a good bicycle fit, every cyclist is unique. We share some common patterns, but how each of us is built and how we choose to ride matter.

I've long wavered in my ability to call myself a cyclist. Sure, I ride a bike almost every day, but "cyclist" rarely seemed like the right word to describe me. True, I've spent numerous hours in the saddle, but a cyclist seemed like someone fitter, faster, more professional, and, frankly, male. When my friends started using the term to introduce me—as in "This is Laura—she's a big cyclist"—I would find ways to disclaim it, saying, "Oh, I just ride around the city a lot." Why has it been so hard for me to own this title?

I've felt this way about a number of roles: cyclist, Bostonian, Christian. A few years back, I visited a friend in another city. He had his two bikes for us to adventure on, but he was about six inches taller than I am. On the bike I was riding, we put the seat as low as it could go. Then I leaned the frame to the side so I could throw my leg over the top tube and try to pop onto the saddle. My hands stretched far in front of me to reach the handlebars. I managed to pedal, but during the whole ride, I felt unstable. The bike was too big for me, like the poor fit of these roles.

I've lived in Boston or Cambridge for fifteen years now, and yet I've most often said, "I'm from New Jersey, but I live in Boston." The title of "Bostonian" seemed to belong to someone who had more history in this place than I did. Yet, riding through the city formed me as a Bostonian, over years of tracing the cow paths of Boston's streets until they became my own. My bicycle accelerated my acceptance of this place.

It's uncomfortable to claim titles and roles that other people have taken on before us. In owning the public role of a Christian, I was hesitant because of the negative associations many people have. A whole bunch of badly behaving Christians makes the rest of us nervous about claiming the name ourselves.

All of this ambivalence and ill fit is a reminder of the public roles we play. Like it or not, when I blow through a stoplight, I give other cyclists a bad reputation. When I'm rude to a clueless driver, I give other Christians a bad name. And when I presume that all roads lead to Boston, I confirm the stereotype of Bostonians' smug assurance that we are indeed the hub of the universe. As ill-fitting as they sometimes are, I have a responsibility to shape these roles, too.

I began to really ride a bicycle as an adult about the same time I was ordained as a Christian pastor, both roles inviting an assent to new identities. Both vocations have uniforms of sorts that mark us as part of a particular tribe. When I started riding my pink-and-gray commuter bike, I took the car license plate stamped "CLERGY" that some pastors use when making hospital visits and serving in emergencies and zip-tied it to my bike rack. I mostly did it as a joke, reveling in the ridiculousness of it. But then it became a recognizable sign. When I commuted with this bike, I knew I was on duty. Friends started calling my ride "ClergyBike."

I've learned the sign does a number of things for me and for others.

The ClergyBike sign works first on me. It's a good social control that reminds me not to behave like a jerk. And I genuinely do feel an increased responsibility to show love and kindness while on ClergyBike. When I'm riding it, I'm representing something larger than myself, and I want to take that responsibility seriously.

I also realize that the city sees my sign—I'm no longer anonymous. People know who I am, and I know that other people know whom I am, in ways that hold me accountable.

The distinctiveness of the ClergyBike also makes me known to others. New conversations with other cyclists tend to start with a bit more familiarity. "So you're the person who rides this bike! I've seen it parked all over the city." A number of times lately, other cyclists have recognized my bike and me from bike blessings and ghost bike dedications. I've also had pedestrians call out to me from the sidewalk, people who recognized me from community events. When I was stopped at a light on Columbus Avenue one day, a man shouted, "Hey, Rev, it's Mike from the 9/11 memorial!" "Hi, Mike!" I shouted back, not entirely sure who he was, as I pedaled off with the light change. I'm especially fond of pulling up alongside bus stops and watching older ladies look perplexed and then smile as they read the sign.

The way I read the Gospels, Jesus spends more time wandering out on the road than he does sequestered away in a religious building. He spends a significant amount of time chatting with people along the dusty roads. He goes to the people, rather than waiting for the people to come to him.

Brother Lawrence, a deeply devout man, believed that we need not be in church to be with God. When we practice the presence of God, our hearts become a mobile prayer room, with us wherever we travel.

If this Christian life is really one where love is stronger than hate and life is stronger than death, I want it visible and recognizable out on the road, not tucked away in some building. I want this fierce love to be seen in all parts of the city. Is there any better way to travel the city roads, in a visible and accessible way, than by bike?

The bicycle is not a universally welcome sign. And not everyone is as amused and convinced by my ClergyBike as I am. About a year ago I rode my bike to a funeral, and stealthily switched shoes and freshened up before walking into the church. Later, I heard through the swift channels of church gossip that some people thought this was undignified. That suggests a lingering perception that bikes are toys for children, and those of us who continue to ride are stuck in some sort of cycling adolescence. Or there's a perception that if we were really adults, with adult jobs and adult salaries, we would own cars. Whatever these grumbling people were thinking, they didn't positively associate bicycles with funerals.

Riding a bike and claiming to be a cyclist signify different things in different places. In some parts of the world and the U.S., riding a bicycle implies poverty, while driving a car denotes modernity and upward social mobility. Attempting to ride his bike around Las Vegas, musician and cyclist David Byrne deduced, "The only other people on bikes there were people who had lost everything, probably to gambling. They'd lost their jobs, families, houses, and I guess—ultimate insult for an American—their car." While riding his bicycle in rural Wales, cyclist Robert Penn was repeatedly cornered in the pub by people convinced that he must have lost his driver's license to drunk driving. Why else would he ride a bike rather than take a car? "For a Welsh farmer there could be no other reason."

Riding a bicycle as primary transportation isn't something massively countercultural in many parts of the world. But in the U.S., with the overwhelming normativity of our car culture, the choice to ride a bike stands out. And with that visibility comes the weight of assumptions and projections.

Most Americans assume that cycling is a choice rather than an economic necessity. If you're a cyclist, they may assume that you're some squishy environmentalist fueled by quinoa and smugness. They may also assume you're stuck in adolescence and not a real grown-up. And they may project behaviors onto you based on the worst scofflaw cyclist they've ever seen on the road, regardless of how fastidious you are in obeying the rules.

Despite all of the projections about who we are and the assumptions about why we ride, one truth of our cycling cannot be covered over or blotted out: Cyclists have fun.

It's a simple but powerful fact: Riding a bike is fun.

What was a chore has been turned into delight. Maybe those assumptions about delayed adulthood hold some truth, as cyclists get to recall a childhood thrill put to the service of adult transportation. There's a playfulness that even an adult experiences when riding a bike. When was the last time you heard a motorist brag about how much fun they had during their morning commute? At best, it seems, motorists and those who take the bus and the train can hope for efficiency; fun never even seems to enter the realm of possibility.

Moving swiftly under the power of our own legs, cyclists have a freedom few other travelers enjoy. The assumption that a car is the quickest and most convenient form of transportation doesn't hold up in urban transit. In the city, I can often get around faster by bike. I almost never struggle to find a parking spot. My upkeep costs are lower than those of maintaining a car. And it's far more enjoyable to be zipping along Massachusetts Avenue on a bike instead of sitting in gridlock, stewing in my anger and exhaust fumes. Even when the traffic is jammed up and the road appears blocked, I can generally find a way through on my bike. When I do, I feel strong, capable—and joyful.

Despite all the cautionary tales I've told about getting doored and getting yelled at, I also experience goodness and grace on the road. There's a cost to cycling regularly, but the payout is joy.

If happiness is temporary and conditional, joy is the deep truth that transcends any one occasion or circumstance. I believe life on a bicycle cultivates a practice of joy. I can have a slow ride home, get passed by some disrespectful cyclists, get shouted at by some angry motorists, and end up damp from the rain, but still sustain the joy of being on my bicycle and the prospect of a better ride tomorrow.

I've come to believe that joy is as much an urban spiritual discipline as rest, and border-crossing, and attentiveness. Joy is the practice of seeing nature in its seasons—not just the trees barren and cold in winter but full and flourishing in spring. Joy is the practice of seeing not just the despair and decay of the city, but intentionally and carefully looking for small signs of life. The discipline of joy requires not merely seeing the dirty streets, but learning to look for the small man tucked in the doorway, hidden in the shadow, broom in hand, ready to sweep away the dust.

Joy comes from aligning our lives as best we can with the deepest values to which we aspire, and from believing that holiness is all around us. Joy cuts against the reputed dourness of the religious life. After all, this way of being in the world is supposed to be *good* news.

I do not ride because it is my duty. I do not ride merely because it is practical. I ride because the bicycle brings me joy.

No doubt it's possible to ride grumpily and dutifully. It's possible to scowl the entire length of your commute and turn the whole thing into another act of drudgery. But the mere act of placing your feet on the pedals and pushing away so that you feel the wind in your face and the sun on your skin makes it hard to be a grouch for too long. I can ride angry, and I have. But the very act of riding itself seems to work out some of that thunder.

I've often experienced this transformation on my regular route home. If I'm willing to chat with other cyclists, I can get out of my funk and get to delight in neighbors I'd likely never meet otherwise. Over my cycling years, I've met an Argentinian sous chef coming home from a late shift, a cardio-thoracic surgeon who commutes to the hospitals, and an earnest young man attending college in Boston, far from home in California.

Once I even found myself riding in the rain with Boston's then "bike czar," who happened to be an Olympic cyclist. We may ride together for only a few miles, but our bikes—and the joy of riding them in each other's company—bind us together.

Bicycle joy is also mine regardless of what others do around me. No rude cyclist or motorist can take away my joy unless I hand it over to them. Others can insult me or endanger me, cut me off and curse me, but it is my choice to stay peaceful or get angry. Only I can surrender my joy of life on a bike. In this way, joy is a spiritual discipline just like every other one—something to be practiced, cultivated, nurtured, and shared. Like the decision to take a bike over a car, I make the daily decision to practice joy.

Running late to a meeting recently, I pedaled faster to try to make up some time, which doesn't work especially well on a bike commute. Every intersection foiled me. Every pothole seemed bigger than the day before. Every light seemed to turn red just before I arrived. And my hands were turning red, too, because it was cold and I'd forgotten my gloves on the dining table. I was busy stewing in my own self-pity and frustration when I saw a young cyclist coming towards me. On his way up the hill, this boy had popped a wheelie, twisting and wiggling to keep moving forward without dropping his front tire. His eyes were fixed in concentration, but as soon as he saw me, he broke into a full-mouthed grin. I shouted "Impressive!" as we passed each other, and I rang my bell a few times in admiration. I could have kept stewing, cold and cranky, all the way to my inane meeting. But why not receive another cyclist's invitation to the joy of life on a bicycle?

That joy is most easily found not in isolation, but in the community of the city—and the cycling community knows this. Every month in every kind of weather, on the second Friday of the month, the Boston Bike Party takes over the city streets. Their purpose is not protest, but joy. As many as five hundred people show up to go on the adventure of a free and public group ride through the city. During the ride, which is entirely volunteer-run, some cyclists pull trailers with speakers blasting music, and others ride in costumes. And there's always a giant dance party along the way. Boston Bike Partiers are effusive evangelists for the joy of two-wheeled travel. They aren't riding toward a destination, but for the sheer delight of traveling together.

And once a year, we get a foretaste of that heavenly city where the roads are not violent, but open and gentle. "Hub on Wheels" is the annual group ride of thousands, when Boston officials shut down our busiest streets. Roads previously forbidden to bikes are suddenly all ours. The four-lane highway of Storrow Drive, usually an aggressive slalom course where buses threaten to wipe out cars on every curve, becomes a meandering wide boulevard where cyclists can ride along the Charles River. Children in bike-trailers coast alongside tandem cyclists in matching tweed outfits, next to roadies in Spandex and tourists on the Hubway bike share. From every corner of the city, we ride together, and for a few hours, we know that the streets can be joyful and kind.

There is joy everywhere on the road, even the mean streets of Boston on a regular day, if we cultivate the eyes to see and the ears to hear. Like most other commuters, I've been conditioned to travel with my guard up. I've even developed a typology of which travelers will be the most infuriating. Motorists in fancy cars seem to be less cautious and behave in a more entitled way. Taxis and ride shares are trouble. I've learned to avoid big trucks, since they rarely have an expansive enough view to see me. Big SUVs can be a problem, too. Hybrid cars, though small and earth-friendly, can be a challenge because they operate in stealth mode: their silent engines mess with my ability to gauge how close vehicles are to me based on their rumble. And then there are pick-up trucks. Most of the time, I haven't thought of them as cyclist-friendly co-users of the road.

But that impression changed for me one night after work. I was biking from my office to the Boston Children's Hospital at Longwood Medical Center to pay a visit to another pastor whose child had just been admitted. Having successfully navigated through the swirling pit of death where all roads converge at Kenmore Square into a knot of cars, I picked up Brookline Avenue past Fenway where it crosses over Park Drive. At rush hour, the car traffic was jammed up, but the bike lane was fairly clear. When I merged back into traffic to take a left onto Longwood Avenue, a dirty pick-up truck with a surly-looking driver pulled up alongside of me on my right. I could feel my body tense as the man rolled down his window and stuck his head out.

"Hey, Pastor," he shouted over the rush-hour noise, with a Boston accent that made it sound more like "Pasta." "Hey, Pasta," he shouted again as I turned my head towards him. "Does that make you a holy roller?" He grinned with glee. I stood confused at the red light; I had steeled myself for an insult. But he didn't wait for me to make sense of the moment. "Get it?" he shouted, his left hand pointing at the clergy sign on my bike rack. "A holy roller!" The light changed to green, and I could hear him laughing as he drove off.

The road has conditioned me to expect an insult instead of a joke. But a discipline of joy holds out the hope for something more. When I practice this way of life, it increases the possibility I might just find it.

Brother Lawrence, though quite advanced in his spiritual practice, sought to be a "perpetual novice." He had a sense that there is always something more to learn, always another facet of God to explore. Cyclists find this true of bicycles. There is always more to know, but one primary thing to remember: a bike requires forward motion. For a bicycle to stay upright, it has to keep moving. Even the hipster cyclist badge of honor known as a "trackstand," a trick of keeping the bike upright and still while balancing on the pedals, is actually created by the cyclist's small movements rocking forward and back.

Writing to another spiritual seeker, Brother Lawrence counseled, "We must always continue to labor, since in the life of the spirit, not to advance is to fall back." Life on a bicycle has taught me to keep moving forward, but at a more reasonable pace. By bike, I have learned a spiritual discipline of prayer and contemplation of my city. By bike, I have connected with people and places previously unknown to me.

We keep moving forward, like the young cyclist pedaling uphill, seeing if he can't do something even more creative, even more adventurous. Life on a bike has given me the sheer gladness of being a fellow cyclist in this holy city, a joy worth changing my life for.

Every morning I lug my bike up the stairs from the basement, from below the cool earth into the day. Brushing against the too-close chain-link fence, I walk over a small patch of grass to where the concrete sidewalk begins. Down the curb, through the parked cars, and onto the pavement, I maneuver my bicycle out into the city street.

With my saddle firmly under me, I stretch my hands forward and raise my eyes to the horizon. My left foot is poised at the top of the stroke in anticipation. As soon as my right foot pushes off from the ground, the forward movement begins.

What I see, where I go, and the power to get there is dependent on me. This isn't flying. I don't leave the earth, but move more joyfully across it. I don't know what will meet me on the road, but delight is always possible. I always move forward on a bike.

There is always an unexplored neighborhood somewhere in the city.

There is always more of the infinite mystery of the Holy to explore.

There is always a new road to ride.

Blessing of the Bicycles Service

Note: We've held this service in a range of locations in Boston, but the front stairs outside of the church seem to work best. The Cathedral of St. John the Divine in New York City holds their massive blessing inside the church, with bicycles down the aisles. This service has been adapted and refined over several years, initially based on the service at House for All Saints and Sinners in Denver, Colorado. You can adapt it to suit the needs of your city and its cycling community. The following text is suggested, not required.

To download this version, please go to RevEverett.com.

Materials Checklist:

- Printed orders of the service
- Table
- Lectern
- Microphones
- Anointing oil/chain lube
- Small dishes
- Hand towels
- Helmets for collecting the offering

Order of Service

Introduction to the Blessing of the Bicycles

Dearly gathered velocipedes and those who love them,
We are gathered here today to bless our bicycles, these sacred machines that weave our way through Boston's tangled streets.
We welcome you to this holy act whoever you are, and however you got here.
You are welcome, all you deist, theist, agnostic bikes. We welcome all you Christian, Jewish, Buddhist, Hindu, and Muslim bikes.
You are welcome, all you tricycles, you who believe in the Trinity.
You are welcome, all you bicycles, you who believe in the fully human and fully divine.
You are welcome, all you unicycles, you who believe in the radical oneness of God.
We welcome you whether you believe a little or believe a lot. We welcome you whether you ride a little or ride a lot.
Whoever you are, wherever you are on your spiritual journey, and whatever kind of bike you ride, you are welcome here.

Opening Song (adapted)

Oh, when the saints come riding in,
Oh, when the saints come riding in,
Lord I want to be in that number
When the saints come riding in.

Oh, when our bells begin to ring [ring bike bells!],
Oh, when our bells begin to ring,

Oh, how I want to be in that number
When our bells begin to ring.

Oh, when the light turns red to green,
Oh, when the light turns red to green,
Oh, how I want to be in that number
When the light turns red to green.

Oh, when the road is safe for all,
Oh, when the road is safe for all,
Oh, how I want to be in that number
When the road is safe for all.

Reading

A reading from the Prophet Ezekiel, the first chapter:

"The living creatures darted to and fro, like a flash of lightning. . . . When the living creatures moved, the wheels moved beside them; and when the living creatures rose from the earth, the wheels rose. Wherever the spirit would go, they went, and the wheels rose along with them; for the spirit of the living creatures was in the wheels. When they moved, the others moved; when they stopped, the others stopped; and when they rose from the earth, the wheels rose along with them; for the spirit of the living creatures was in the wheels."

Prayers of the People

Riding a bicycle is a spiritual discipline. We could take the subway; we could take a car. But no. We gear up, putting on base layers, balaclavas, and booties. We stash that spare change of clothes, taking over bathroom stalls and emerging like superheroes. Riding a bicycle is a spiritual discipline. And all of you should be praised for the decision you make every day to live more sustainably, move more freely, love more deeply. You know the deep joy of life on a bike.

And yet, for as much joy as there is in riding a bicycle, there is so much struggle. We see a secret Boston, missed in a car or on the train. We see the same guys living outside through this cruel winter and then suddenly gone. We see the foreclosed houses and the lonely people. We see accidents, and crime scenes, and roadside memorials.

We take this time to name that which lies heavy on our hearts each day as we take our bikes on the road. I will end each petition by saying "Holy One." Please respond by saying, "Hear our prayer." Let us pray:

Present in a world groaning under the excesses of consumption, we acknowledge the inherent goodness of non-motorized, human-powered transportation and give thanks for the simple beauty of the bicycle. Holy One, *Hear our prayer.*

Present in our community filled with children and adults, we pray for those learning to ride. Keep them smart, safe, and visible on our neighborhood roads. Holy One, *Hear our prayer.*

Present in a community filled with strife, we pray for the victims of road rage and bike theft. We ask for the strength to forgive mean people. Forgive our impatience. Holy One, *Hear our prayer.*

Present in a world of work, we pray for those who build, repair, and clean our bikes and those who rely on bicycles to earn their living. Bless the Boston Cyclists Union and all who advocate for a more just and sustainable future. Bless those who choose not to drive and those for whom driving isn't even an option. Holy One, *Hear our prayer.*

Present in a community of beautiful diversity, we ask your protection and blessing on all who ride: pedi-cabbies and weekend warriors; commuters and messengers; Freds and roadies and Hubway tourists; the old and the young; biking believers and questioners; and all who take to the Boston streets, paths, parks, and hills. Keep us safe as we ride. Holy One, *Hear our prayer.*

Let us hold a moment of silence for all who have died in Greater Boston while on bicycles in the past year, remembering _____.

And those whose names are known to God alone. May God comfort all who mourn and restore the broken-hearted. Holy One, *Hear our prayer.* Let the people say, *Amen.*

Blessing of the Bicycles

We will bless the bicycles like this: We invite you to merge into two lanes of traffic. Roll your bike forward, and we will bless your bike, or your helmet, or you too. We will put a little anointing oil mixed with chain lube on you to bless you and say:

Bless, protect, and guide this bicycle. May love be always in your heart and the wind be always at your back. *Amen.*

Offering

At this point we take up an offering, collected in helmets, to support the Survivors' Fund. The Boston Cyclists Union works with survivors, family members, and friends after every incident to keep them engaged with the work of "Vision Zero," the day when there are zero fatalities on Boston's streets.

A Word of Gratitude

We use this time to allow local cyclists to offer a word of thanks or testimony about why they ride and why they come to have their bicycles blessed. This is also a good time to thank any elected officials, bicycle cops, and supporting houses of worship.

Closing Song: "This Little Light of Mine" (adapted)

This little light of mine, I'm going to let it shine.
This little light of mine, I'm going to let it shine.
This little light of mine, I'm going to let it shine.
Let it shine, let it shine, let it shine.

All around the neighborhood, I'm going to let it shine.
All around the neighborhood, I'm going to let it shine.
All around the neighborhood, I'm going to let it shine.
Let it shine, let it shine, let it shine.

Hide it under a helmet? No! I'm going to let it shine.
Hide it under a helmet? No! I'm going to let it shine.
Hide it under a helmet? No! I'm going to let it shine.
Let it shine, let it shine, let it shine.

Don't let the headwind blow it out!
 I'm going to let it shine.
Don't let the headwind blow it out!
 I'm going to let it shine.
Don't let the headwind blow it out!
 I'm going to let it shine.
Let it shine, let it shine, let it shine.

Benediction

As you depart, receive this blessing:

 May the road rise up to meet you.
 May the wind always be at your back.
 May the sun shine warm upon your face,
 and rains fall soft upon your roads.
 And until we meet again,
 May God hold you in the palm of his hand.

Now go forth in peace and joy! Ring your bells and say *Amen!*

Ghost Bike Service

This is only a template for a ghost bike service. I've learned, time and time again, that each service is as distinct as the individual, and needs to be appropriate for the context and community gathered. In my experience, the crowd that turns out for a ghost bike service will likely not have a common set of songs or prayers or sacred readings. So I've often used Psalm 23 and a poem chosen for each person as the sacred "texts." Sometimes we sing some-

thing easily teachable, like "Meditation on Breathing" by Sarah Dan Jones, or something well known, like "Amazing Grace."

I've also found that people really need a shared ritual to grieve a death like this, so at the end of the service, I invite them to come forward and touch the bicycle and bless it themselves. Sometimes we've held this service as a candlelight vigil, passing out lit candles at the beginning and inviting cyclists to leave them at the ghost bike at the end. Sometimes I've invited people to take a ribbon to tie on their bikes in honor of the deceased cyclist and as a reminder that they too are worthy to be seen. I've also invited people in advance to bring flowers to place next to the ghost bike. I've learned to print more copies of the service than I expect to need—people seem to want to have something tangible to take home.

When elected officials attend, I've learned to acknowledge them publicly, but in order to keep the ceremony an appropriate memorial and not a rally, I don't invite them to speak. I do try to line up some readers in advance for the story of Ghost Bikes and the readings, and some volunteers to take up the collection. We've often had a leader from the "Ride of Silence," a national commemorative ride, introduce the "Moment of Silence."

Feel free to adapt the service, but please do give credit to Rev. Laura Everett, Boston, MA. Directions on how to make and install a ghost bike can be found at http://ghostbikes.org/howto. To download this version, please go to RevEverett.com.

Memorial for _____ and Installation of a Ghost Bike

Welcome & Introduction

Dear cyclists and you who loved _____, welcome.
We are gathered here today to dedicate a ghost bike, a visible

sign of an invisible reality—that we are fragile humans, only here for a little while.

We are here to make a visible sign of a dawning awareness— that we must peacefully coexist on these shared Boston roads for all of us to stay alive.

We are here to honor _____'s life, to pray for all who grieve her death, to rededicate ourselves to the day when there are zero fatalities on Boston's roads, when Boston is a peaceable city, not paved with gold but with protected cycle tracks.

We welcome you to this holy act, whoever you are and how- ever you got here.

You are welcome here, whatever you believe. You are welcome here, whatever you feel this night.

You are welcome here if you bring your anger, your grief, your sorrow. You are welcome here if you bring your despair, your rage, your resignation. Whoever you are, however you got here, whatever you are feeling, you are welcome here on this holy ground. This place is made holy by _____'s life, and by your presence. You need bring nothing other than yourself. It is good and right that you are here, however you come. By being present here, you honor _____'s life and her death. By being pres- ent here, together we proclaim with our bodies and our bicycles that _____'s death will not go unnoticed. Thank you. Thank you for being here so that we do not grieve alone.

Together this evening, we'll hear a few readings, hear from _____'s community and fellow cyclists, and dedicate this ghost bike.

[Optional: We want to acknowledge the elected and city offi- cials who have joined us. Thank you for being here.]

The Story of Ghost Bikes

During this time, a leader in the cycling community tells the origin story of ghost bikes. We find this a helpful way of grounding this tradition in our history and educating new cyclists and the media who might not have seen a ritual like this before.

Today, we participate in a ritual that happens all over the world. Ghost bikes began in St. Louis in 2003, when Patrick Van Der Tuin, a young man in his mid-twenties, "saw a car drift into a bike lane and hit a female cyclist from behind. Her injuries were minor, but the incident stuck with him."[*] The accident was not far from his home, just a block away. He passed it daily as he rode his own bike. As he passed the scene of the accident again and again, he developed an idea. Patrick "got his hands on a bunch of junk bikes, painted them white, and started combing police reports for locations of bike accidents and fatalities."[**] The original installation was called "Broken Bikes, Broken Lives." That first ghost bike didn't last twenty-four hours. It was quickly taken down.

A few years later, in Pittsburgh, a small group of cyclists picked up the idea from St. Louis and coined the term "ghost bike." A cyclist named Eric Boerer had himself been hit by a car, and his leg was badly broken. "We had a meeting around a picnic table," he remembers, "basically drinking beers and trying to brainstorm ideas on this project. Someone mentioned 'ghost bikes,' because of the connotation that the bikes are gone and they're ghosts of bikes. Part of it also was that we kind of thought peo-

[*] http://grist.org/living/the-story-of-ghost-bikes-how-a-bike-memorial-in-st-louis-sparked-a-global-movement/.
[**] http://grist.org/living/the-story-of-ghost-bikes-how-a-bike-memorial-in-st-louis-sparked-a-global-movement/.

ple saw through us, almost looked at us as ghosts on the streets, like they didn't really pay attention to us. We were almost invisible in a way."*

By installing a ghost bike here, at this dangerous intersection, we make visible _____'s life, and _____'s death. Here we offer a visible reminder that cyclists need not be invisible. We are worthy to be seen.

Reading: Psalm 23   Reader: _____

The Lord is my shepherd, I shall not want.
    He makes me lie down in green pastures;
he leads me beside still waters;
    he restores my soul.
He leads me in right paths
    for his name's sake.

Even though I walk through the darkest valley,
    I fear no evil;
for you are with me;
    your rod and your staff—
    they comfort me.

You prepare a table before me
    in the presence of my enemies;
you anoint my head with oil;
    my cup overflows.
Surely goodness and mercy shall follow me
    all the days of my life,
and I shall dwell in the house of the Lord
    my whole life long.

* http://grist.org/living/the-story-of-ghost-bikes-how-a-bike-memorial-in-st-louis-sparked-a-global-movement/.

Poem: _____   *Reader:* _____

At the ghost bike ceremonies, we try to include many people from the community. Before each dedication, I select a poem to be read that relates to the life and the passions of the deceased.

Reading

I also add a reading if we have access to an essay, a blog post, or something else the deceased has written. It can be helpful and profound for the gathered community to hear their words again. It's important to remember that many of the cyclists who turn out for these ghost bike dedications may not know the deceased, so hearing their own words helps familiarize the gathered community.

Remembering _____

All who knew and mourn _____'s death are invited to share a brief memory or hope. (*This is the "open mic" portion of the service to memorialize the deceased. I try to stand next to the speaker, both to provide support and to keep things moving.*)

Prayers of the People

Each petition of the prayer I will offer ends with "Holy One." Please respond by saying, "Hear our prayer."

Will you pray with me?

Holy One, we call you by many names: Creator God, Higher Power, Love that never ends, The Wind that is always at our back.

Many roads brought us safely here, to this small square of earth. We stand and ride on holy ground. We gather in grief to remember a life well lived, a life too short, possibilities unfulfilled. As we gather in our grief, Holy One, *Hear our prayer.*

We praise you for the life of _____ and for the time they spent in this place. We give thanks for [name some characteristics of the deceased]. As we give thanks for the life of _____, Holy One, *Hear our prayer.*

When we chose to take a bike instead of a car,

when we chose to listen instead of shout,

when we chose advocacy instead of complacency,

when we chose to get curious instead of cranky,

when we chose to heal a broken world instead of cursing it,

when we travel past this spot,

remind us of _____. Holy One, *Hear our prayer.*

We remember the names of those who have died while riding in Boston over the past year: _____.

Comfort all who mourn this day. Holy One, *Hear our prayer.*

We weep and rage with all who were present at the crash. We remember those who witnessed things no one should see, and the ambient trauma to neighbors, commuters, first responders, and workers in [location]. May the images fade from your eyes and the noise ebb in your ears. As our community suffers, Holy One, *Hear our prayer.*

We who continue to ride these roads confess that some days we ride scared, some days we ride angry. Here, on this holy ground, we pray and recommit ourselves to work for a day when all people will be safe on these streets. Holy One, *Hear our prayer.*

We pray for our cities, for Boston, for Cambridge, for every bridge and every person that moves across and in-between. We long for a day when "Death will be no more; mourning and crying and pain will be no more." Wipe every tear from our eyes. Holy One, *Hear our prayer. Amen.*

Moment of Silence

Someone needs to introduce this, to tell people you will hold a moment of silence for one minute. We've used a bike bell to designate the beginning and the end. After all the preceding talking, sometimes silence helps.

Dedication of the Ghost Bike

Friends, if you'd like, I invite you to gather around as we dedicate _____'s ghost bike. Get close with one another. Come touch the bicycle, or ask if you can place a hand on someone else touching the bicycle.

Let us pray:

On this holy ground, we dedicate and bless this ghost bike. May all who look upon it be reminded of the awesome responsibility of driving cars and trucks. May this ghost bike be a sign and a promise. May it be a sign of our fragile lives on these roads. May it be a promise that _____'s life and legacy will not be lost. Bless this memorial to _____. And bless us, too.

Let the people say, *Amen.*

Offering

This is the point at which we pass bike helmets to collect an offering for a ghost bike memorial fund, administered by the local cycling advocacy organization.

Benediction

As you leave, hear this benediction:

May the road rise up to meet you.
May the wind always be at your back.
May the sun shine warm upon your face,
and rains fall soft upon your roads.
And until we meet again,
May God hold you in the palm of his hand.

Blessing the Ghost Bike

As you leave, I invite you to place your hands on the ghost bike and perhaps say:

> "I give thanks for the life of _____. May all who look on this ghost bike remember _____ and travel with care."

Notes

Notes to the Introduction

1 **"Cyclists escape the pain and drudgery"**: Bike Snob NYC, *Bike Snob: Systematically and Mercilessly Realigning the World of Cycling* (San Francisco: Chronicle Books, 2010), p. 49.
5 **"rush hour is ripe for a messiah"**: Bike Snob NYC, *The Enlightened Cyclist*, p. 31.
5 **"Today I ride to get to work"**: Robert Penn, *It's All about the Bike: The Pursuit of Happiness on Two Wheels* (New York: Bloomsbury, 2010), p. 11.

Notes to Chapter 1

9 **"There is no manner of life in the world sweeter"**: Brother Lawrence of the Resurrection, *The Practice of the Presence of God* (Brewster, MA: Paraclete Press, 2010), p. 55.
10 **Prior to around 1896, an average bicycle cost**: Robert Smith, *A Social History of the Bicycle* (New York: McGraw-Hill, 1972), p. 13.
10 **"the vast majority of early cyclists in America"**: Robert Hurst, *The Art of Urban Cycling: Lessons from the Street* (Guilford, CT: Globe Pequot Press, 2004), p. 11.
11 **"for opponents of women's rights, the bicycle"**: Lorenz J. Finison, *Boston's Cycling Craze, 1880-1900: A Story of Race, Sport, and Society* (Boston: University of Massachusetts Press, 2014), p. 68.
13 **"The word 'rule' derives from a Latin word"**: http://ssje.org/5.pdf/cowleypdf/2011%20Summer%20Insert.pdf.
15 **"You may have as many asses"**: Brother Lawrence of the Resurrection, *The Practice of the Presence of God*, p. 55.

Notes

15 **"continual conversation with God"**: Brother Lawrence of the Resurrection, *The Practice of the Presence of God*, p. 55.

19 **He counsels the seeker to "think often" about God**: Brother Lawrence of the Resurrection, *The Practice of the Presence of God*, p. 75.

Notes to Chapter 2

20 **"She would like to go more quickly"**: Brother Lawrence of the Resurrection, *The Practice of the Presence of God* (Brewster, MA: Paraclete Press, 2010), p. 73.

22 **"Look at the birds of the air"**: Matthew 6:26.

27 **"We must not be surprised at failing"**: Brother Lawrence of the Resurrection, *The Practice of the Presence of God*, p. 46.

31 **"make a searching and fearless moral inventory"**: http://www.aa.org/assets/en_US/en_step4.pdf.

32 **"will give a bumpy ride even on a smooth road"**: http://sheldonbrown.com/gloss tp- z.html#true.

32 **"All penance and other spiritual practices"**: Brother Lawrence of the Resurrection, *The Practice of the Presence of God*, p. 39.

32 **"watch attentively over all movements"**: Brother Lawrence of the Resurrection, *The Practice of the Presence of God*, pp. 32-33.

Notes to Chapter 3

35 **"Get accustomed to suffering"**: Brother Lawrence of the Resurrection, *The Practice of the Presence of God* (Brewster, MA: Paraclete Press, 2010), p. 77.

38 **"The threat of tens of thousands"**: Robert Penn, *It's All about the Bike: The Pursuit of Happiness on Two Wheels* (New York: Bloomsbury, 2010), p. 164.

38 **"improves with use"**: Penn, *It's All about the Bike*, pp. 171-72.

Notes to Chapter 4

43 **"He called the practice of the presence of God"**: Brother Lawrence of the Resurrection, *The Practice of the Presence of God* (Brewster, MA: Paraclete Press, 2010), p. 13.

52 **When I look at the 1936 Federal Housing Administration map**: http://hyperallergic.com/238667/artists-and-activists-trace-bostons-historic-red-line-on-the-streets/.

181

Notes to Chapter 5

55 **"The goal of all his [Brother Lawrence's] actions"**: Brother Lawrence of the Resurrection, *The Practice of the Presence of God* (Brewster, MA: Paraclete Press, 2010), p. 35.

56 **"an enlightened commuter defers"**: Bike Snob NYC, *The Enlightened Cyclist: Commuter Angst, Dangerous Drivers, and Other Obstacles on the Path to Two-Wheeled Transcendence* (San Francisco: Chronicle Books, 2012), p. 100.

56 **"Cars kill, whereas bicycles mostly just annoy"**: Bike Snob NYC, *The Enlightened Cyclist*, p. 94.

60 **"God's instructions to Noah"**: Bike Snob NYC, *The Enlightened Cyclist*, p. 44.

61 **Cycling advocacy groups speak of "invisible cyclists"**: Andrew Keatts, *Governing*, October 26, 2015. http://www.governing.com/topics/transportation-infrastructure/memo-to-cities-most-cyclists-arent-urban-hipsters.html.

65 **Begun in St. Louis in 2003**: http://grist.org/living/the-story-of-ghost-bikes-how-a-bike-memorial-in-st-louis-sparked-a-global-movement/70.

70 **Though our ranks have tripled in the past decade**: http://www.bostonglobe.com/metro/2015/10/20/census-biking-work-increasingly-popular-boston/3W6yUSXUSHey7X1bCr3fYL/story.html.

70 **And among the city's cyclists, women**:http://www.cityofboston.gov/Lyris/Images/BostonBikeCountPresentation-dfb90c.png.

Notes to Chapter 6

71 **"I advise you not to pray aloud"**: Brother Lawrence of the Resurrection, *The Practice of the Presence of God* (Brewster, MA: Paraclete Press, 2010), p. 71.

75 **For a time, the national League**: Lorenz J. Finison, *Boston's Cycling Craze, 1880-1900: A Story of Race, Sport, and Society* (Boston, MA: University of Massachusetts Press, 2014), p. 193.

76 **"Workmen who have bicycles"**: Finison, *Boston's Cycling Craze*, p. 194.

76 **"God delights in every innocent pleasure"**: Finison, *Boston's Cycling Craze*, p. 194.

78 **"My God, I adore you in my infirmities"**: Brother Lawrence of the Resurrection, *The Practice of the Presence of God*, p. 25.

79 **"we must behave very simply with God"**: Brother Lawrence of the Resurrection, *The Practice of the Presence of God*, p. 37.

Notes

82 **"so familiar that he used to say"**: Brother Lawrence of the Resurrection, *The Practice of the Presence of God*, p. 116.

82 **"I possess God as tranquility"**: Brother Lawrence of the Resurrection, *The Practice of the Presence of God*, p. 116.

83 **"We do not have to be constantly in church"**: Brother Lawrence of the Resurrection, *The Practice of the Presence of God*, p. 59 (language for God adapted).

Notes to Chapter 7

84 **"He had fulfilled his kitchen duties"**: Brother Lawrence of the Resurrection, *The Practice of the Presence of God* (Brewster, MA: Paraclete Press, 2010), pp. 13-14.

87 **"Light, strong, cheap—pick any two"**: Bike Snob NYC, *The Enlightened Cyclist: Commuter Angst, Dangerous Drivers, and Other Obstacles on the Path to Two-Wheeled Transcendence* (San Francisco: Chronicle Books, 2012), p. 155.

87 **"You can sit up with your hands on the flat 'tops'"**: Robert Penn, *It's All about the Bike: The Pursuit of Happiness on Two Wheels* (New York: Bloomsbury, 2010), p. 72.

93 **"Instead of stopping behind you"**: Bike Snob NYC, *The Enlightened Cyclist*, p. 67.

94 **"not having bells on their bikes"**: Bike Snob NYC, *The Enlightened Cyclist*, p. 126.

94 **"painful-looking pratfalls as he crashed"**: Sean Patrick Farrell, "When Bikers Clash, the Tape Rolls," *The New York Times*, June 24, 2011. http://www.nytimes.com/2011/06/26/nyregion/more-urban-bike-disputes-are-caught-on-video.html.

95 **Initially, everyone seemed onboard**: Jim Vrabel, *A People's History of the New Boston* (Boston: University of Massachusetts Press, 2014), p. 140.

96 **As people had organized and strategized**: Vrabel, *A People's History of the New Boston*, p. 147.

96 **"You can't build an enormous eight-lane super-road"**: Vrabel, *A People's History of the New Boston*, p. 140.

96 **"promised he wouldn't 'make decisions'"**: Vrabel, *A People's History of the New Boston*, p. 146.

Notes to Chapter 8

98 **"Although his duties were great and difficult"**: Brother Lawrence of the Resurrection, *The Practice of the Presence of God* (Brewster, MA: Paraclete Press, 2010), p. 13.

100 **"Variable gears are only for people over forty-five"**: Robert Penn, *It's All about the Bike: The Pursuit of Happiness on Two Wheels* (New York: Bloomsbury, 2010), p. 98.

100 **"Riding a single speed can help bring back"**: Sheldon Brown. http://www.sheldonbrown.com/singlespeed.html.

101 **"one-ness with the bike that is not equaled"**: Sheldon Brown. http://www.sheldonbrown.com/singlespeed.html.

101 **"Riding one [a brakeless fixie] well in city traffic"**: Robert Hurst, *The Art of Urban Cycling: Lessons from the Street* (Guilford, CT: Globe Pequot Press, 2004), p. 217.

104 **"The key to proper shifting is thinking ahead"**: Mike Cusionbury, "Tips from the Pros: The Key to Sublime Shifting, Says Mountain Bike Pro Andreas Hestler, Is Finding the Sweet Spot," *Bicycling Magazine*, June 27, 2010. http://www.bicycling.com/training/bike-skills/tips-pros.

105 **The Retro-Grouch has "passionate respect"**: Bike Snob NYC, *Bike Snob: Systematically and Mercilessly Realigning the World of Cycling* (San Francisco: Chronicle Books, 2010), p. 76.

106 **"at least ten to fifteen years to make sure"**: Bike Snob NYC, *Bike Snob*, p. 77.

106 **"Cyclists fare best when they"**: John Forester, *Effective Cycling*, 7th ed. (Cambridge, MA: MIT Press, 2012), p. 19.

110 **"Make straight the way of the Lord"**: Mark 1:3.

110 **"Every valley shall be filled"**: Luke 3:5-6.

111 **"As the architect of the cycling canon"**: Blog post, Bike Snob NYC, February 5, 2008: "Thanks, Sheldon." http://bikesnobnyc.blogspot.com/2008/02/thanks-sheldon05.html.

111 **According to his website, he fielded**: Here's the website address: http://bikesnobnyc.blogspot.com/2008/02/thanks-sheldon_05.html.

111 **Sheldon's *Boston Globe* obituary dubbed him a "cyber-sage"**: Ross Kerber, "Homespun Wisdom: Beloved Newton Bike-Shop Mechanic, Cyber-Sage Sheldon Brown Will Be Missed," *Boston Globe*, February 8, 2008. http://archive.boston.com/news/local/articles/2008/02/08/homepsun_wisdom/.

Notes to Chapter 9

114 **"He lifted himself up to God"**: Brother Lawrence of the Resurrection, *The Practice of the Presence of God* (Brewster, MA: Paraclete Press, 2010), pp. 16-17, adapted.

118 **"The good brother found God everywhere"**: Brother Lawrence of the Resurrection, *The Practice of the Presence of God*, p. 120.

119 **In working with interfaith gatherings**: At a 1985 press conference in

Notes

Stockholm, Lutheran Bishop Krister Stendahl coined the term "Holy Envy" as one of his three rules for interfaith understanding. Stendahl suggested that we "leave room for holy envy" of another's religious traditions.

124 **"silent, secret, nearly unbroken conversation"**: Brother Lawrence of the Resurrection, *The Practice of the Presence of God*, p. 63.

Notes to Chapter 10

125 **"Even though by nature he had a great aversion"**: Brother Lawrence of the Resurrection, *The Practice of the Presence of God* (Brewster, MA: Paraclete Press, 2010), pp. 37-38.

126 **The earliest "helmets" were**: Randy Swart, "The History of Bicycle Helmets," Bicycle Helmet Safety Institute. http://www.bhsi.org/history .htm.

126 **"bicycle helmets provide significant protection"**: Robert Hurst, *The Art of Urban Cycling: Lessons from the Street* (Guilford, CT: Globe Pequot Press, 2004), pp. 167-68.

126 **Even though most cycling deaths involve**: Jeff Mapes, *Pedaling Revolution: How Cyclists Are Changing American Cities* (Corvallis, OR: Oregon State University Press, 2009), p. 224.

127 **Mandatory helmet laws in parts of Australia**: Mapes, *Pedaling Revolution*, p. 224.

127 **"Statistically, an hour of driving"**: Hurst, *The Art of Urban Cycling*, p. 171.

130 **For Brother Lawrence, the continual conversation**: Brother Lawrence of the Resurrection, *The Practice of the Presence of God*, p. 45.

132 **"I can imagine that for people of color"**: Jeremy Dowsett, "What My Bike Has Taught Me about White Privilege," August 20, 2014. http:// alittlemoresauce.com/2014/08/20/what-my-bike-has-taught-me-about -white-privilege/.

132 **"The experience I [as a white man] have as a cyclist"**: Jeremy Dowsett, "My Bike and White Privilege, Revisited," September 11, 2014. http://alittlemoresauce.com/2014/09/11/my-bike-and-white -privilege-revisited/.

135 **"We have not loved you with our whole heart"**: *Prayer Book and Hymnal containing the Book of Common Prayer and the Hymnal, 1982 according to the Use of the Episcopal Church* (New York: Church Publishing Incorporated, 1986), p. 360.

Notes to Chapter 11

137 **"We cannot avoid the dangers and reefs"**: Brother Lawrence of the Resurrection, *The Practice of the Presence of God* (Brewster, MA: Paraclete Press, 2010), p. 74, adapted.

138 **"Panic stops are a symptom of cyclists' mistakes"**: Robert Hurst, *The Art of Urban Cycling: Lessons from the Street* (Guilford, CT: Globe Pequot Press, 2004), p. 129.

139 **"It is better to anticipate problems"**: Hurst, *The Art of Urban Cycling*, p. 129.

141 **Such extremes make me wonder**: Bianca Barragan, "16 Comparisons to Show Exactly How Enormous Los Angeles Is," Monday, March 23, 2015. http://la.curbed.com/2015/3/23/9977854/how-big-is-los-angeles.

144 **"When he failed, he did nothing but admit his fault"**: Brother Lawrence of the Resurrection, *The Practice of the Presence of God*, p. 37.

147 **If we do, then we've unconsciously adopted a "Sports Utility Vehicle theology"**: Carol Johnston, "Thinking Theologically about Wealth, including Money," p. 5. http://www.resourcingchristianity.org/sites/default/files/transcripts/research_article/CarolJohnston_Thinking_Theologically_About_Wealth_Essay.pdf.

Notes to Chapter 12

149 **"We do not have to be constantly at church"**: Brother Lawrence of the Resurrection, *The Practice of the Presence of God* (Brewster, MA: Paraclete Press, 2010), p. 59.

150 **"However, we must always continue to labor"**: Brother Lawrence of the Resurrection, *The Practice of the Presence of God*, p. 53.

154 **"The only other people on bikes"**: David Byrne, *Bicycle Diaries* (London: Viking Penguin, 2009), p. 77.

154 **"For a Welsh farmer there could be no other reason"**: Robert Penn, *It's All about the Bike: The Pursuit of Happiness on Two Wheels* (New York: Bloomsbury, 2010), pp. 14–15.

160 **Brother Lawrence, though quite advanced**: Brother Lawrence of the Resurrection, *The Practice of the Presence of God*, p. 39.

Acknowledgments

It's a scary thing to put one's heart on paper for the world to see. Many people convinced me I could, and it wouldn't be awful. I am grateful for them, because they made this book possible.

This book is a team effort. In writing, as in cycling, we go further together.

As I said, I am grateful for many, including the following groups and individuals:

The amazing team at Eerdmans, including Lil Copan, who helped dream up and enflesh this project; Mary Hietbrink, who patiently helped me clarify my thoughts and coach me through; and Amanda Skofstad and Rachel Bomberger, who cheered me over the finish line. I'd ride with you ladies any day, and twice on Sunday.

Angela Baggetta and Golderberg McDuffie Communications. It's a complicated thing to promote one's self. You encourage me to believe that I have a story worth telling.

Paul Soupiset, whose illustrations made this book. Thank you for seeing both the beauty and the heartbreak in our cities.

Alex and Jerelyn Wilson, my cousins, who shared their home as a writing retreat and model a values-driven, sustainable life.

The Brothers of the Society of St. John the Evangelist in Cambridge, Massachusetts. Your rule of life compels me, and your commitment to the city inspires me. Thank you for opening your hearts and doors to me and so many others.

Rev. Dr. Almeda Wright, a fabulous teacher, a sharp mind, and a steady writing partner. Thank you for your companionship, friend.

Rev. Gregory Morisse. You are a sure sign of God's provision. Your support bolsters me, and your love buffers me.

The encyclopedic Erich Leas, who served as the resident bike geek on this book, and all-around cheerleader.

Boston's cycling community—you alive, vibrant, defiantly joyful people, you. Thank God for the Boston Bike Party, Hub on Wheels, the Boston Cyclists Union, Bike Talks, Mass Bike, Femmechanics, and the "tactical urbanists" who prompt us to change unsafe roads. Together we're building a more joyful and more just city.

The bicycle shops that have been spaces for me to learn, especially Hub Bicycle with Emily Thibodeau, Bowdoin Bike School with Noah and Jovanny De Amor, Bikes Not Bombs, International Bicycle, and Landry's.

Acknowledgments

Team Monster Truck and friends from Cannoli Friday. Thank you to Josh, Emily, Val, Dana, Cxy Dan, Jessie, Tim, Kristen, Hila, Matt, Erich, Franko, Eric, Nathaniel, David, Galen, Pete, John, Greg, Ella, and Paolo. We practiced joy together.

The members of Boston's Ghost Bike Planning Committee, especially John, Peter, Joel, Jonathan, Christine, Jon, Lumina, Michelle, Daniela, Matt, Doug, Becca, Lee, Phil, Ken, Anne Marie, Jessie, Jessica, Rebecca, Laura, Patrick, Richard, and many others. You all teach me to honor the dead and repair the road.

The Boston Faith & Justice Network, who held that economic discipleship Bible study at the time my car died. Thank you for helping me, and many others, try to live more justly and faithfully with our money. Thank you to Hope Central Church, and every church that blesses bikes. Thank you to the church-lady bike sherpas, who blaze a trail: Angela, Sandy, Trinity, Judy, Marisa, and Abbi. Ride on in majesty.

Leadership Education at Duke Divinity School, especially Dave Odom, Craig Dykstra, Greg Jones, Kelly Gilmer, Sally Hicks, Maria Teresa Gastón, Gretchen Ziegenhals, Victoria White, and all of the ridiculously smart colleagues at Convocation. Thank you for taking me on, and encouraging me to write.

The friends who themselves have written fabulous books and coached me through, especially Mike Martin and Ellen Goldstein, Chapin Garner, Keith Anderson, Adrian Miller, Dan Kennedy, and Ken Evers-Hood.

Colleagues through the Massachusetts Council of Churches. You've granted me the time and the space to write, and you've

189

only giggled a little when I show up to a church event decked out in a neon jacket and bike shoes. I believe in what we do together.

The powerful alumna of Brown University and the women of my book club. You make me brave and challenge me to do more to repair this broken world.

The Christ Clarion clergy group and the Boston clergy ladies. You make me strive to be a better pastor.

My parents, Rick and Mary Everett, who first put me on a bike and gave me a good push into the world. Thank you for teaching me to ride, trusting me to navigate my own way, and cheering me on.

And finally,

My sister, Kate. We're a long way from the back streets of NJ. Being your sister makes the journey so much better. We can travel hard roads together. You teach me to claim my space and ring my own bell.

And my beloved Abbi. I had no idea that repairing a hand-me-down bicycle with you would lead me down this road, and I could not be happier. Thank you for sharing your love, and your love of bicycles with me. May we ride side by side, all the days of our lives.

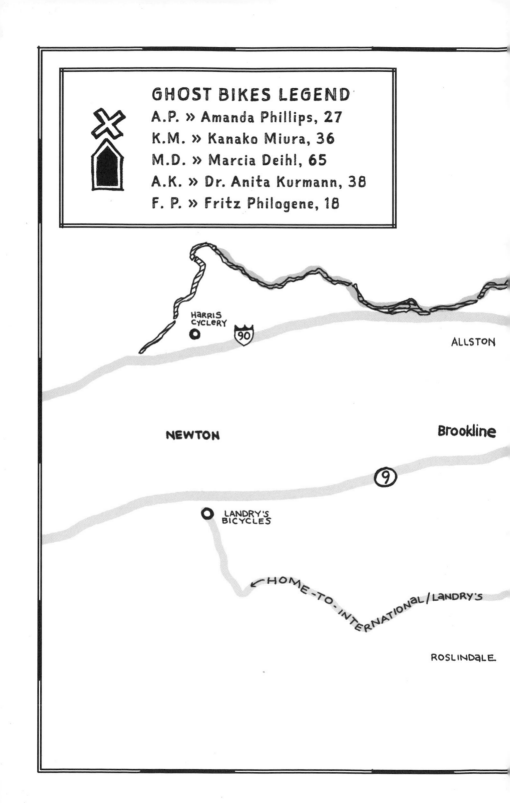

GHOST BIKES LEGEND
A.P. » Amanda Phillips, 27
K.M. » Kanako Miura, 36
M.D. » Marcia Deihl, 65
A.K. » Dr. Anita Kurmann, 38
F. P. » Fritz Philogene, 18

HaRRiS CYCLeRY

90

ALLSTON

NEWTON

Brookline

9

LANDRY'S BICYCLES

HOME-TO-INTERNATIONAL/LaNDRY'S

ROSLINDaLE